Study Guide to Accompany

CRIMINAL INVESTIGATION

THIRD EDITION

Bruce L. Berg
Department of Criminal Justice
California State University

John J. Horga
Special Agent, Retired
Federal Bureau of Investigation

D1307168

**Glencoe
McGraw-Hill**

New York, New York   Columbus, Ohio   Woodland Hills, California   Peoria, Illinois

Glencoe/McGraw-Hill

A Division of The **McGraw-Hill** *Companies*

Study Guide for *Criminal Investigation,* Third Edition

Send all inquiries to:

Glencoe/McGraw-Hill
936 Eastwind Drive
Westerville, OH 43081

ISBN 0-02-800931-2

Printed in the United States of America

4 5 6 7 8 9 0 QSR/QSR 0 9 8 7 6 5

CONTENTS

To the Student

This study guide is intended to assist you in understanding the concepts presented in *Criminal Investigation,* Third Edition, by Bruce L. Berg and John J. Horgan. This study guide will help you review the subject material and test yourself on your grasp of the material. As well, this study guide provides an opportunity for practicing and applying the concepts presented in the text. To effectively complete the exercises in this study guide you must first carefully read the chapter material.

Study Outline

The fill-in outline at the beginning of each chapter provides a summary of the major topics and issues discussed in the corresponding textbook chapter. This section tests your recall of the material being presented and also indicates areas where you may lack complete recognition of certain concepts. An answer key is not provided for this exercise. Answers are easily found in your text.

Concept Review

This section reviews your understanding of the concepts and principles presented in the text through a series of True/False statements. If you find that, after reading the textbook chapter, you have difficulty deciding which statements are true or false, you should reread the chapter. Answers for this section are provided in the Answer Key at the back of this study guide.

Key Terms Review

This section reviews your understanding of the major terms and concepts presented in the chapter. The matching exercise helps you identify the key terms you should be familiar with after studying the chapter. Try to answer this section without relying on your textbook. Answers for this section are provided in the Answer Key.

Applying Concepts

This section provides you the opportunity to apply the concepts you have learned to investigative situations. You will exercise your newly acquired investigative and critical thinking skills while applying the principles of criminal investigation. Answers are provided in the Answer Key.

Career Development

This section offers an overview of some of the careers available in the field of criminal justice where investigative techniques are used. It also offers some tips on developing résumés and preparing for job interviews.

How to Use This Study Guide

1. Study the Chapter Objectives at the beginning of each chapter to become familiar with the concepts that will be presented in the chapter.

2. Review the list of Key Terms to learn which investigative terms and phrases are important to know.

3. Skim the chapter to note the heading structure, look at the photographs and captions, and briefly study the figures.

4. Read the chapter carefully using one of the following methods of textbook reading:
   a. Outlining
   b. Writing marginal questions
   c. Highlighting
   d. Mapping
   e. SQ4R (Survey, Question, Read, Recite, (W)rite, Review)

5. Reread the Chapter Objectives at the beginning of the chapter and then review the Summary at the end of each chapter.

6. Answer the Questions for Review at the end of the chapter.

7. Complete the Critical Thinking and Investigative Skill Builder exercises at the end of the chapter.

8. Complete the Study Outline in this study guide. Try to complete it without the help of your textbook. If you cannot complete a fill-in item, look it up in your textbook.

9. Next complete the Concept Review, Key Terms Review, and Applying Concepts sections without your textbook. Check your answers with the Answer Key.

10. Review any concepts, terms, or principles that you are unsure of.

CHAPTER 1 Basic Grounding and Overview

Study Outline

What Is Crime?

1. Sutherland and Cressey suggest four primary factors related to understanding whether a _____ is a crime.

2. The purpose of criminal law is to prevent _____ to society.

3. At one time, most people considered crime a _____.

4. Each crime must have an exact _____.

5. Crimes in the United States are defined in the following bodies of law: _____,

_____, _____, _____, and

_____.

6. Crimes may be divided into two broad categories according to the severity of the criminal behavior: _felonies_ and _misdemeanors_

What Is Criminal Investigation?

1. Criminal investigation is a _usually initiated by personal observation or infamation from A citizen_

2. The primary objectives of a criminal investigation are the following:
   a. _measuring_   I. _questioning victims, witness + suspects_
   b. _photographing_   J. _recading all statements_
   c. _video taping_   K. _Observation in notes,_
   d. _Sketching the scene_
   e. _Searching for evidence_
   f. _identifying_
   g. _Collecting_
   h. _examing + processing phipical evidence_

Pg 34

3. Most of the procedural, or due-process, rights of criminal suspects in the United States are prescribed

   in the _____.

Requisites of a Successful Criminal Investigator

1. _____ reasoning is the drawing of conclusions from logically related events or observations.

2. _____ reasoning moves from particular and apparently separate observations or pieces

   of information or evidence.

Concept Review

For each statement, write **T** *in the space provided if the entire statement is true. Write* **F** *if any part of the statement is false.*

___F___ 1. Crime can be defined only in the dictionary.

___F___ 2. Crime today is considered a private matter.

___T___ 3. Crimes are defined in several different bodies of law.

___F___ 4. Case law originated in England.

___F___ 5. The United States Constitution has little to do with laws protecting Americans.

___T___ 6. The Bill of Rights was not originally part of the U.S. Constitution.

___T___ 7. Felonies are more serious crimes than misdemeanors.

___F___ 8. Criminal investigators use only inductive reasoning.

___F___ 9. Murder is a misdemeanor under federal law.

___T___ 10. Administrative and regulatory law are essentially the same thing.

Key Terms Review

Match the terms with the definitions. Write the letter of the term in the answer column.

a. case law
b. procedural law
c. misdemeanor
d. prosecutor
e. deductive reasoning
f. common law
g. crime
h. criminal investigation
i. penal code

j. administrative law
k. due process of law
l. defendant
m. precedent
n. substantive law
o. criminal law
p. statutory law
q. inductive reasoning
r. felony

_G_ 1. An offense against the public at large, proclaimed in a law and punishable by a governing body.

_O_ 2. The body of law that, for the purpose of preventing harm to society, defines what behavior is criminal and prescribes the punishment to be imposed for such behavior.

_D_ 3. Name given to the government as the party that accuses a person of a crime.

_L_ 4. In criminal law, the person who is accused of a crime.

_F_ 5. Principles and rules of action based on usage and custom in ancient England and incorporated into colonial American laws and subsequent state statutes.

_P_ 6. The body of laws passed by legislative bodies, including the U.S. Congress, state legislatures, and local governing bodies.

_i_ 7. A collection of state statutes that define criminal offenses and specify corresponding fines and punishments.

_A_ 8. The sum total of all reported cases that interpret previous decisions, statutes, regulations, and constitutional provisions that then become part of a nation's or a state's common law.

_m_ 9. A decision in a court case that furnishes an example or authority for deciding subsequent cases in which identical or similar facts are presented.

_J_ 10. The body of law created by administrative agencies in the form of rules, regulations, orders, and decisions, sometimes with criminal penalties for violations.

_R_ 11. A relatively serious criminal offense punishable by death or by imprisonment for more than a year in a state or federal prison.

_C_ 12. A less serious crime that is generally punishable by a prison sentence of not more than one year in a county or city jail.

_H_ 13. The lawful search for people and things to reconstruct the circumstances of an illegal act, apprehend or determine the guilty party, and aid in the state's prosecution of the offender.

_N_ 14. The body of law that creates, defines, and regulates rights and defines crime and its penalties.

_B_ 15. The body of law that prescribes the manner or method by which rights and responsibilities may be exercised and enforced.

_K_ 16. The rights of people suspected of or charged with crimes, prescribed by the U.S. Constitution, state constitutions, and federal and state statutes.

_E_ 17. The drawing of conclusions from logically related events or observations.

_Q_ 18. The making of inferences from apparently separate observations or pieces of evidence.

Applying Concepts

1. For each of the following, determine whether the logical sequence is a model of **deduction** or **induction.**

    a. An officer enters a room and finds a man standing over the bleeding body of a woman. The man is holding a knife, which is dripping with blood. The officer concludes that the man has stabbed the woman.

    ____✓____ Deduction   _____ Induction

    b. An officer receives a call to a domestic disturbance. Upon arriving, she finds a man lying asleep on the couch and a woman washing dishes in the kitchen. Two children are calmly watching television. The officer concludes that the call for a domestic disturbance was an error.

    _____ Deduction   ____✓____ Induction

    c. An officer answers a call for a robbery in progress at a local delicatessen. He arrives to find two people outside pointing toward an alley, shouting, "Officer, the robbers ran down there!" Without checking with the merchant, the officer concludes that the robbers have run down the alley.

    _____ Deduction   ____✓____ Induction

2. For each of the preceding scenarios, explain what the officer should have done before drawing any conclusion.

    a. _____

    _____

    _____

    _____

    _____

    _____

    b. _____

    _____

    _____

    _____

    _____

    _____

    c. _____

    _____

    _____

    _____

    _____

    _____

CHAPTER 2   The Preliminary Investigation

Study Outline

Initial Response

1. The fact-gathering activities that take place at the scene of a crime after it has been reported or

   discovered are all part of the _____.

2. Uniformed officers arriving on the scene of a crime must use their _____
   to assess what is going on.

3. *Corpus delicti* represents basic elements of an offense, specifically _____

   _____.

4. Sometimes, the *corpus delicti* of a crime can be apparent on the face of the evidence, or

   _____.

5. A preliminary investigation may be the prelude to a(n) _____

   _____.

6. The _____ and teamwork between patrol officers and detectives might be compared to a baseball game.

The Crime Scene

1. The first responsibility of any law enforcement officer is to _____

   _____.

2. As soon as possible after arriving on the scene, officers usually determine _____

   _____.

3. When the officer arrives at a crime scene, he or she must decide on a plan of _____.

4. Investigative activities at the crime scene should include the following:

   a. _____

   b. _____

   c. _____

   d. _____

e. _____

f. _____

g. _____

h. _____

5. To make identification of suspects easier, officers sometimes use a _____,
   in which a witness notes physical similarities between the suspect and another person.

6. When suspects are taken into custody, they usually are given a(n) _____
   informing them of their rights.

Recording the Crime Scene

1. List three reasons why note taking is critically important in a criminal investigation:

   a. _____

   b. _____

   c. _____

2. Accurate field notes should answer these six questions: _____, _____,

   _____, _____, _____, and _____.

3. Field notes are the major frame of reference and raw source from which _____

   _____ are prepared.

The Legal Significance of Evidence

1. If an investigating officer determines that a criminal law has been violated, the _____

   _____ of the particular crime must be established.

2. Sometimes the facts of a crime can be established by _____
   evidence, evidence that is good and sufficient on its face.

3. Criminal investigators must have a working knowledge of the _____
   to ensure that evidence collected will be admissible in court.

4. The three tests of the admissibility of evidence are _____, _____, and

   _____.

Concept Review

For each statement, write **T** *in the space provided if the entire statement is true. Write* **F** *if any part of the statement is false.*

___T___ 1. In most crimes reported to or discovered by police, investigative activities are initially undertaken by uniformed patrol officers.

___T___ 2. Some calls to the police require immediate action, while other calls may not.

___F___ 3. The *corpus delicti* of a crime is not important for criminal investigations.

___F___ 4. The term *prima facie* refers to the type of crime committed.

___F___ 5. Circumstantial evidence cannot be used to secure a conviction.

___T___ 6. In larger departments, detectives usually conduct follow-up investigations.

___T___ 7. At a crime scene, the first thing an officer should do is determine if anyone is injured.

___F___ 8. Even if an officer believes there is nothing to do to save an injured person, he or she should not leave to pursue a fleeing felon.

___F___ 9. The exclusionary rule sets the standard of admissibility against which evidence is judged.

___T___ 10. Most arrests are actually made without an arrest warrant.

___T___ 11. Just about anything can be admitted in court as evidence, provided there is no rule that prohibits its being admitted.

___F___ 12. A composite description allows the witness to look at a person whose height is known and note the similarities and differences between that person and the suspect.

___F___ 13. Field notes are an optional element in criminal investigations.

___F___ 14. Finished field notes need only be approximate, with just enough detail to make sense to the officer recording them.

___T___ 15. A good investigative report should include the location, disposition, and name of the finder of each item of evidence.

___T___ 16. Radio dispatchers should be advised of needs for assistance at a crime scene as soon as possible.

___F___ 17. The crime scene should be secured as soon as possible to prevent the media from knowing too much.

___T___ 18. The proportion of cases that result in an arrest at the crime scene is rather small.

___T___ 19. Anyone with knowledge of the crime should be identified and should be separated from others with knowledge of the crime.

___F___ 20. *Corpus delicti* is the physical evidence found at the crime scene.

Key Terms Review

Match the terms with the definitions. Write the letter of the term in the answer column.

a.	composite description	**i.**	*Miranda* warning
b.	materiality	**j.**	exclusionary rule
c.	*prima facie* evidence	**k.**	competency
d.	preliminary investigation	**l.**	chain of custody
e.	hot pursuit	**m.**	relevancy
f.	rules of evidence	**n.**	custody
g.	dying declaration	**o.**	circumstantial evidence
h.	comparison description	**p.**	*corpus delicti*

___D___   **1.** Fact-gathering activities that take place at the scene of a crime immediately after the crime has been reported to or discovered by police officers.

___G___   **2.** A statement given by a victim at a crime scene, in anticipation of death. It is admissible as evidence.

___H___   **3.** A physical description in which a victim or witness notes similarities and differences between the suspect and another person, whose characteristics are known.

___A___   **4.** A description obtained by compiling separate, slightly varying descriptions into a whole.

___I___   **5.** A cautionary statement to suspects in police custody, advising them of their rights to remain silent and to have an attorney present during interrogation.

___N___   **6.** Detainment by a police officer; a situation in which a person feels he or she is not free to leave.

___E___   **7.** The crossing of jurisdictional lines to chase a suspect.

___L___   **8.** Proof of the possession of evidence from the moment it is found until the moment it is offered in evidence.

___P___   **9.** All the material facts showing that a crime has been committed; Latin for "body of the crime."

___C___   **10.** Evidence good and sufficient on its face to establish a given fact or chain of facts and, if not rebutted or contradicted, to be proof of that fact; Latin for "on the surface."

___O___   **11.** Evidence of other facts from which deductions can be drawn to show indirectly the facts to be proved.

___F___   **12.** Rules of court that govern the admissibility of evidence at trials and hearings.

___J___   **13.** The rule that evidence that has been obtained in violation of constitutional guarantees against unlawful search and seizure cannot be used at trial.

___m___   **14.** The applicability of evidence in determining the truth or falsity of the issue being tried; a requirement for admissibility in court.

___B___   **15.** The importance of evidence in influencing the court's opinion because of its connection with the issue; a requirement for admissibility in court.

___K___   **16.** The quality of evidence, or its fitness to be presented to assist in determining questions of fact; a requirement for admissibility in court; also used to describe a witness as legally fit and qualified to give testimony.

Applying Concepts

1. You are an officer in a single-officer patrol car cruising the main drag of a small city. Over your radio you receive a call to back up Officer Johnson, who is checking out a suspicious car parked in the Winn-Dixie supermarket parking lot. As you drive into the lot, you see Officer Johnson approaching the parked car. Suddenly, you hear two shots fired and see Officer Johnson fall to the ground. You also see the suspect car speeding away to the north exit from the parking lot and turning right onto Oak Street. What actions will you take? Explain your answer.

_____

_____

_____

_____

_____

_____

_____

_____

_____

_____

_____

_____

_____

_____

_____

_____

_____

_____

_____

_____

2. Two officers obtain an arrest warrant for a man suspected of raping an 11-year-old girl. They arrive at the man's residence and identify the suspect. The officers place handcuffs on the suspect and seat him in their patrol car. During the 10-minute ride to the station, the officers repeatedly call the man names and ask why he raped the girl. Finally, with tears in his eyes, the suspect shouts that she was always walking around in skimpy outfits and that she was nothing but a filthy little tease who deserved to be raped. He admits having raped her, as well as her best friend from down the street—someone the police were not aware was involved.

In spite of his confession in the car, the man pleads not guilty and never signs any confession. In court, the victim has difficulty answering certain questions posed by the defense counsel, and the other little girl refuses to come forward. The defendant is found not guilty because of insufficient evidence. How is this possible?

_____

_____

_____

_____

_____

_____

_____

_____

_____

_____

_____

_____

_____

_____

_____

_____

_____

_____

_____

CHAPTER 3   Preserving the Crime Scene

Study Outline

Evidence and the Crime Scene

1. In a criminal investigation, _____ is any item that helps to establish the facts of a related criminal case.

2. To aid in the search for evidence, some investigators call on _____, who are persons specifically trained to collect and assess physical evidence.

3. There are eight basic procedures that the investigator should keep in mind when gathering and preserving evidence at a crime scene:

    a. _____

    b. _____

    c. _____

    d. _____

    e. _____

    f. _____

    g. _____

    h. _____

4. The _____ can be understood to include all areas in which the criminal, any possible victim, and any eyewitnesses moved during the time the crime was committed.

Pictorial Documentation of the Crime Scene

1. Photographs should be taken of the crime scene only, without _____.

2. One guideline for taking crime scene photographs is to progress from the general to the specific, using three

    major vantage points: _____, _____,

    and _____.

3. Sometimes, it may be necessary to include a(n) _____ to help viewers understand the size and distance relationships depicted in the photograph.

4. Photographs or videotapes taken at a crime scene should be identified by a _____

      _____.

Sketching the Crime Scene

1. While photographs provide exacting details, sketches offer accurate information about _____

      _____.

2. All measurements of a sketch should be accurate in scale, to prevent _____

      _____.

3. Legally, for a sketch or diagram to be admissible in court, it must meet the following requirements:

    a. _____

    b. _____

    c. _____

4. Several methods can be used to prepare crime scene sketches. They include:

    a. _____

    b. _____

    c. _____

    d. _____

    e. _____

Discovering and Recognizing Evidence

1. Depending on the location of the crime scene, investigators may choose one of the following five basic search patterns:

    a. _____

    b. _____

    c. _____

    d. _____

    e. _____

2. The _____ and _____ search patterns are the ones most commonly used by investigators.

Collecting and Marking Evidence

1. In considering evidence, the court will want answers to the following questions about its collection:

   a. Who _____

   b. What _____

   c. When _____

   d. Where _____

   e. Where _____

2. Some types of evidence, such as fingerprints, require a(n) _____,
   or a model, measure, or object with which the evidence is compared.

Concept Review

For each statement, write **T** *in the space provided if the entire statement is true. Write* **F** *if any part of the statement is false.*

___F___ 1. The crime scene includes only the immediate area where the suspect is arrested.

___T___ 2. Nothing at the crime scene should be touched, altered, or moved until it has been identified, photographed, measured, and recorded.

___F___ 3. To accomplish a spiral search, the investigator stands in the middle of the area to be searched and turns counterclockwise to scan the area.

___F___ 4. Sketching and photographing major crime scenes is optional.

___T___ 5. Cross projection is one method of showing the location of objects in a crime scene sketch.

___F___ 6. The zone search patterns involves imagining a series of lanes dividing up the entire area to be searched.

___T___ 7. When evidence is found, the investigator should place his or her mark on it.

___T___ 8. Latex gloves are useful equipment for patrol officers to carry in their cruisers.

___T___ 9. During the actual process of collecting evidence, care must be taken not to destroy or contaminate any evidence.

___F___ 10. To accomplish a strip search, an investigator must divide the area to be searched into four quadrants.

Key Terms Review

Match the terms with the definitions. Write the letter of the term in the answer column.

a. spiral search pattern
b. rectangular-coordinates method
c. pie, or wheel, search pattern
d. compass point method
e. criminalist
f. grid search pattern
g. triangulation method

h. standard of comparison
i. evidence
j. cross projection method
k. strip search pattern
l. zone search pattern
m. baseline method

___I___ 1. Any item that helps to establish the facts of a related criminal case. It may be found at the scene of the crime or on the victim or taken from the suspect or the suspect's environment.

___E___ 2. A person specifically trained to collect evidence and to make scientific tests and assessments of various types of physical evidence.

___B___ 3. A sketching method that involves measuring the distance of an object from two fixed lines at right angles to each other. It is often used to locate objects in a room.

___G___ 4. A sketching method that requires measuring the distance of an object along a straight line from two widely separated, fixed reference points.

___m___ 5. A sketching method that takes measurements along and from a single reference line, which can be established by using a length of string, a chalk line, or some other convenient means.

___D___ 6. A sketching method that requires a protractor or some other method of measuring angles between two lines. One point is selected as the origin, and a line extending from the origin becomes an axis from which angles can be measured.

___J___ 7. A sketching method in which the ceiling appears to open up like the lid of a hinged box, with the four walls opening outward. Measurements are then indicated from a point on the floor to the wall.

___A___ 8. A search pattern typically used in outdoor areas and normally launched by a single person. He or she begins in the outermost corner and walks in a decreasing spiral toward a central point.

___K___ 9. A search pattern in which the space to be searched is divided into a series of lanes. One or more searchers proceed up and down each lane, continuing until the area has been completely searched.

___F___ 10. A search pattern that consists of two strip searches, the second perpendicular to the first. It allows the area to be viewed from two angles.

___L___ 11. A search pattern in which the area is divided into four quadrants, each of which is then examined with one of the other patterns.

___C___ 12. A search pattern in which the area is divided into pie-shaped sections, usually six in number. Each section is then searched, usually by a variation of the strip pattern.

___H___ 13. A model, measure, or object with which evidence is compared to determine whether both came from the same source.

Applying Concepts

After reading the facts of the following hypothetical case, describe how you would preserve the crime scene and what types of evidence you would collect.

Case Facts

At 0900 hours the suspect entered a neighborhood grocery store. He then took a shopping cart, and the lone store employee saw him proceeding up and down the store aisles, selecting grocery items. At the time, there were three other customers in the store. The suspect, just prior to the attempted robbery and aggravated assault, was seen picking up a copy of *TV Guide* and casually thumbing through it.

A few minutes later, the suspect approached the checkout counter with several items in his cart. By this time, the other three customers had already made their purchases and left the store. As the store employee began ringing up the items in the suspect's cart, the suspect drew a blue, short-barreled revolver from beneath his mostly green Miami Hurricanes sweatshirt. He leaned over the counter, pressing the gun tight against the neck of the store employee, and said, "Give me all of the bills or I will blow your head off!"

The clerk, who had been robbed several times before and was determined not to let it happen again, pretended to comply but then lunged at the suspect. The suspect struggled with the clerk and, during the skirmish, struck him in the face and head with the gun. The blow to the head drove a deep cut into the clerk's left temple. The blow to the face broke the clerk's nose. He bled profusely but was furious to have been injured. He grabbed the suspect's gun hand and bit deep into his wrist, also drawing blood. The suspect dropped the gun on the counter for a moment, but quickly regained it. He aimed at the clerk and fired one round. The clerk jumped backward and dived behind the counter. From his position on the floor, the clerk could see where the bullet had missed him and ripped into the corner of the counter. The suspect shook his bleeding hand and wailed in pain and frustration. He fired a second shot at the clerk through the counter and then ran from the store without having obtained any money for his trouble.

As the clerk rose from behind the counter, he realized that the wound he had inflicted on the suspect had drawn serious bleeding. There was a trail of large blood drops from the counter through the door. He cautiously glanced out the front window in time to see the suspect getting into a red 1994 Toyota Tercel. As it sped away, the clerk saw it had Texas plates, but he could not make out the numbers.

Walking back to the counter, the clerk saw the suspect's shopping cart. In it were the following items: the *TV Guide* he had been reading, a 2-liter bottle of Fresca, a package of Kraft American cheese, a loaf of bread, and a bottle of mustard.

When the police arrived, the suspect was described as a white male, about 25 years old, 5'9" or 5'10", about 175 pounds, with short, light brown or dirty-blond hair, wearing Western-cut blue jeans, a green Miami Hurricanes sweatshirt with a large pelican (the Hurricanes' mascot) on the front, and black and white patent-leather Air Jordans.

CHAPTER 4   Physical Evidence

Study Outline

The Crime Laboratory

1. Crime laboratories work very closely with _____ and other police personnel in determining whether a crime has actually been committed.

2. The examination carried out in the laboratory can be described in two words: _____ and _____.

3. A crime laboratory is actually a _____ _____ of laboratories under one roof.

4. There are two types of DNA tests. These include _____ (for polymerase chain reaction) and _____ (for restriction fragment length polymorphism).

5. The investigator or technician needs to collect samples that are likely to contain DNA for DNA _____ to be successful.

Blood as Evidence

1. _____ is among the most common forms of evidence found at the scene of serious and violent crimes.

2. Although blood is an excellent form of evidence because of its ability to _____ among individuals, blood can be a serious _____ hazard—regardless of whether it is _____ or dry.

3. Spatters can indicate the _____ of a victim and the perpetrator at the time an attack took place.

4. Blood evidence is useful for _____ suspects as well as for incriminating them.

Semen as Evidence

1. Always handle semen stain areas as _____ as possible.

2. Submit all articles for semen stain examination to the _____ immediately.

Hair as Evidence

1. Hair is a valuable, though sometimes _____, means of personal identification.

2. Sometimes eliminating a suspect is as important as _____ one.

Fibers as Evidence

1. Investigators often overlook fiber evidence because of its extremely _____ size.

2. In many ways, fiber is a better source of information about a crime scene than _____ belonging to the suspect.

Glass as Evidence

1. There are many different _____ used to manufacture glass.

2. Very tiny shards of glass sometimes adhere to a suspect's shoes, _____, hair, or skin.

3. Radial fractures are cracks that start at the _____ of the point where the object struck the glass and _____ outward, creating a slightly star-shaped pattern.

4. Determining the direction of the force that broke the glass involves examining the cone-shaped area created by a _____ fracture.

Paint as Evidence

1. Paint can occur as physical evidence in three different forms. These are:

   a. _____

   b. _____

   c. _____

Firearms/Ammunition as Evidence

1. An important question that may be asked about crimes involving firearms is "Was this _____ fired from this gun?"

2. To assess whether a particular weapon has fired a specific _____, it is necessary to compare the recovered bullet with one _____-_____ through the weapon.

Drugs as Evidence

1. Criminals are often _____ on drugs or _____ when they commit crimes or when they are arrested.

2. From a laboratory examination of drug substances, the following determinations can be made:

   a. _____

   b. _____

   c. _____

Documents as Evidence

1. Handwriting or typefaces may be _____ with other written or printed materials to establish their _____.

2. Documents may contain watermarks or special imprints that can help an investigator identify a distribution or manufacturing _____.

3. Some older printers use _____-_____ technology similar to that of a typewriter.

Concept Review

For each statement, write **T** *in the space provided if the entire statement is true. Write* **F** *if any part of the statement is false.*

_F_ 1. Crime laboratories can be helpful even when no physical evidence is found.

_F_ 2. Dried spills or drops of blood are referred to as globs.

_T_ 3. Even dry blood stains at the crime scene can pose a serious health hazard to investigating officers.

_F_ 4. Hair can identify a suspect as conclusively as a fingerprint.

_T_ 5. The adhesive-tape technique can be used to collect suspected, but not easily visible, fiber evidence.

_F_ 6. Pieces of broken glass are usually not very useful as evidence.

_T_ 7. Paint fragments are sometimes found on the clothing of victims of hit-and-runs.

_T_ 8. Only a physician or other qualified medical professional should remove bullets from the body of a deceased victim.

_T_ 9. Drugs are sometimes a contributing factor in homicides.

_F_ 10. An investigator can handle documents with bare hands, but not other types of evidence.

Key Terms Review

Match the terms with the definitions. Write the letter of the term in the answer column.

a. radial fractures
b. striations
c. reagents
d. concentric fractures
e. bloodstains

f. bore
g. DNA profiling
h. adhesive-tape technique
i. conchoidal fracture
j. blood-typing

G ___ 1. A procedure in which DNA is extracted from biological samples gathered from crime scenes and from comparison samples collected from victims and suspects. The DNA samples are analyzed and compared to determine whether or not they could have had a common origin.

E ___ 2. Dried spills or drops of blood.

C ___ 3. Substances used to detect or test for the presence of blood, or other substances.

J ___ 4. A method of classifying blood into four major blood groups—A, B, AB, and O. Another factor, called the *RH factor*, also determines a person's blood type, which is positive or negative for the Rh factor.

H ___ 5. A method of collecting microscopic evidence by using transparent tape to cover an area to which physical evidence such as fibers may have adhered. When the tape is pulled off, the evidence will adhere to the sticky surface of the tape.

A ___ 6. Cracks that start at the center of the area where an object struck glass and that radiate outward, creating a slightly star-shaped pattern.

D ___ 7. Irregular, but concentric, circular crack patterns in broken glass around the point of impact.

I ___ 8. A series of curved lines along the edge of broken glass that form right angles with one side of the glass, forming a shell- or cone-shaped pattern.

F ___ 9. The hollow, cylindrical chamber, or barrel, of a firearm.

B ___ 10. Marks, lines, or scratches on the surface of an object such as a bullet.

Applying Concepts

On Tuesday night, December 22, 1998, Henry Pullson went out on a date with Genie Martin. The next day, the police arrive at Henry's front door and ask him to identify himself. Henry does so, is read his *Miranda* warnings, and is informed he is under arrest for the rape and murder of Genie Martin.

Genie was found in her apartment, naked on the bed with her throat cut. Medical and laboratory reports indicate that she had recently had forced sex and that traces of sperm were found in her vagina. Also, samples of blood removed from beneath Genie's fingernails were found to be type AB. Genie's blood type was A negative. During preliminary interviews with neighbors, officers learn that Henry and Genie frequently fought and that some sort of loud argument was going on the night she was murdered.

Henry protests his arrest and maintains his innocence. He admits that he and Genie made love, but insists that he used a condom. He also admits that in the past, Genie and he had sometimes argued loudly, but he says they did not on the night of her death. How might we determine whether Henry is a viable suspect in this case?

_____

_____

_____

_____

_____

_____

_____

_____

_____

_____

_____

_____

_____

_____

_____

_____

_____

_____

CHAPTER 5   Criminal Patterns

Study Outline

Crime Patterns and Human Behavior

1. Certain types of criminals commit certain kinds of criminal behavior for similar reasons, or

   _____.

2. The methods and procedures used by a criminal during the commission of his or her crime are called

   the _____, or M.O.

3. Most crimes are motivated by one or a combination of several specific factors, which include the following:

   a. _____

   b. _____

   c. _____

   d. _____

4. Opportunistic crimes require _____ and, therefore, may have no consistent M.O.

Modus Operandi

1. The M.O. file is an orderly method of recording and coding information, designed to reveal

   _____, traits, or practices of criminal suspects.

2. Crimes committed in areas frequented largely by persons working or living in that vicinity usually

   indicate a _____.

3. A suspect with physical disabilities may be eliminated when the type of crime requires an agile person,

   unless evidence of a more physically _____ accomplice is developed.

4. One segment of a suspect's M.O. can have greater value than another for purposes of _____

   _____, _____, or _____.

5. The method of operation can assist in the apprehension of a suspect by pinpointing certain

   _____ patterns.

6. The *modus operandi* parts of a report are generally broken down into 10 or more major subdivisions:

a. _____

b. _____

c. _____

d. _____

e. _____

f. _____

g. _____

h. _____

i. _____

j. _____

7. Terms and initials once thought to be simply tagging, or writing one's nickname or initials as a form

of _____, are now believed to be symbolic gang codes.

Psychological Profiling

1. Psychological profiling is a method of suspect _____ that seeks to identify an individual's mental, emotional, and personality characteristics.

2. Psychological profiles usually begin with a difficult, bizarre, or _____ wave of crime.

3. The physical evidence left at a crime scene often contributes to the development of a

_____ profile of the person who committed the crime.

Concept Review

For each statement, write **T** *in the space provided if the entire statement is true. Write* **F** *if any part of the statement is false.*

___F___ **1.** *Modus operandi* is a French term meaning "methods of operation."

___T___ **2.** The rational-being theory of why people commit crime suggests that some individuals fail to exercise self-control and choose to commit crime as an act of free will.

___T___ **3.** Opportunity is one factor that contributes to the commission of crimes.

___F___ **4.** Having inadequate social skills is not a factor that contributes to the commission of crimes.

___T___ **5.** An M.O. file is an orderly method of recording and coding information designed to reveal habits, traits, and practices of criminal suspects.

___F___ **6.** M.O. information does not assist police in apprehending suspects of crimes.

_F_ **7.** Criminals never select victims because of a particular occupation or class.

_T_ **8.** Symbols drawn on the walls of a crime scene may offer a means of identifying a specific group or cult.

_F_ **9.** Investigators can never introduce the *modus operandi* in a court of law.

_F_ **10.** Psychological profiles are used only in TV and movie versions of police work.

_T_ **11.** Psychological profiling is typically used in crimes of violence, such as homicides, sex crimes, ritualistic or cult crimes, and arson.

_T_ **12.** It was once believed that criminals virtually never changed their M.O.s.

Key Terms Review

Match the terms with the definitions. Write the letter of the term in the answer column.

a. trademark   **f.** *modus operandi* (M.O.)
b. identification   **g.** cults
c. motive   **h.** crime of opportunity
d. psychological profiling   **i.** repression
e. apprehension   **j.** tagging

_C_ **1.** A wrongdoer's reason for committing the crime.

_F_ **2.** The method a criminal uses to commit a crime; Latin term for "mode of operation."

_H_ **3.** A crime that is committed, with little or no planning, as the opportunity presents itself.

_B_ **4.** A process in which physical characteristics and qualities are used to definitely know or recognize a person.

_C_ **5.** The act of seizing or arresting a criminal offender.

_I_ **6.** The act of suppressing or preventing an action from taking place.

_A_ **7.** A distinctive characteristic by which a criminal becomes known.

_J_ **8.** Writing a word or symbol on a wall to identify a person or a group such as a gang.

_D_ **9.** A method of suspect identification that seeks to describe an individual's mental, emotional, and personality characteristics as manifested in things done or left behind at the crime scene.

_G_ **10.** Religious or quasi-religious groups sometimes considered extreme, with followers that sometimes act in an unconventional manner.

Applying Concepts

1. The sheriff's department of a small college town in Florida has been investigating a series of burglaries. The department cannot seem to figure out how to put a stop to them. Below are several brief excerpts from the reports of these burglaries. Using these excerpts, see if you can identify any consistent *modus operandi* that might assist the sheriff's department.

Case A

On Tuesday, December 22, 1998, a suspect entered the victim's apartment at approximately 1300 or 1400 hours. Entry was through the front door, which had been left unlocked. Stereo equipment was taken, including a Panasonic tower stereo with a receiver, tuner, and compact disc player. The system was valued at about $450. Wrapping paper was removed from Christmas presents that the victim had planned to give to relatives, and several gifts were taken. These included a Sanyo portable compact disc player (valued at $100), a 13-inch General Electric color television (valued at $169), and an RCA camcorder (valued at $850). The gifts of books and clothing that were opened were torn and thrown around the apartment. No jewelry was taken, although the victim told police that there were several valuable bracelets and rings in a small jewelry box on top of her dresser.

Case B

On Tuesday, December 8, 1998, a suspect entered the victim's home at approximately 0900 hours. Entry was through a window on the side of the house. A piece of glass had been neatly cut from the pane just above the lock, and the burglar had unlatched and opened the window. Various pieces of artwork were taken, including three limited-edition Sericels of Batman from Warner Brothers Studio. Each was valued at approximately $600. In addition, the victim reported as stolen an 18-inch box-link gold chain (valued at $400); a square onyx ring (valued at $260); a Seiko watch with Mickey Mouse on its face and a gold and silver metal band (valued at $140); two pairs of gold cuff links, one with diamond chips (valued at $125) and one with rubies (valued at $225). The victim also claims to have had stolen $300 in $20 bills, which he had in his sock drawer for emergencies. The victim's new color television and recently purchased stereo equipment were not taken.

Case C

On Thursday, November 26, 1998, a suspect entered the victim's dormitory room at approximately 1400 hours (time was determined because a clock was broken during the crime at 1400 hours). Entry was through the door, which the victim had carelessly left unlocked. Taken in this burglary were a Craig stereo (valued at $250) and an RCA portable compact disc player (valued at $149). The victim's opal ring was not taken and was still on the bookshelf where he had left it. Posters of various rock singers, which the victim had hanging on the walls, had been torn and thrown around the room.

Case D

On Friday, November 20, 1998, a suspect entered the victim's home at approximately 1200 hours to 1300 hours. Entry was made through an open second-floor window, by means of a ladder the victim had left propped against the house (he had been cleaning his gutters earlier in the day). Taken in this burglary were a new 19-inch Zenith color television (valued at $350), a Magnavox VCR (valued at $249), and an RCA portable compact disc player (valued at $149). The victim also complained that two rare and valuable comic books that he had framed and hanging on the wall had been taken down and torn up.

_____

_____

_____

_____

_____

_____

_____

_____

_____

_____

_____

_____

_____

_____

_____

_____

_____

_____

_____

_____

2. How might a psychological profile assist the police in locating a serial killer?

_____

_____

_____

_____

_____

_____

_____

_____

_____

_____

_____

_____

_____

_____

_____

_____

_____

_____

_____

_____

_____

_____

_____

_____

CHAPTER 6   Interviews and Interrogations

Study Outline

Sources of Information

1. Information is the _____ of police work.

2. In its most basic form, an interview may be defined as _____ _____ with a purpose, namely, to gather _____.

3. Sometimes a person being interviewed may say something that causes the officer to believe he or she should actually be a _____.

4. It is important to note that the characterization of interrogations as _____ does not mean that all interviews are conducted with willing participants.

Interviews

1. Rapport is a _____ that develops between an officer and the person being interviewed.

2. Conduct interviews _____ to_____, in a courteous and sincere manner.

3. Separate witnesses, _____ , or others who are to be interviewed about a crime.

4. The _____ interview is a relatively new technique in law enforcement.

5. A complainant is an individual seeking satisfaction or _____ for an injury or for damages sustained.

6. All complaints should be taken _____ until they are demonstrated to have no basis in fact or reality.

7. Complaints are generally divided into two categories:

   a. _____

   b. _____

8. Investigators solve many cases simply by _____ with people and finding out what they may have seen or heard.

9. Ten basic rules for interviewing witnesses are as follows:

a. _____

b. _____

c. _____

d. _____

e. _____

f. _____

g. _____

h. _____

i. _____

j. _____

10. Eyewitnesses are the most important type of _____.

11. Information furnished by children is often _____, and corroborative testimony should always be obtained.

12. If equipment is available, it may be advisable to _____ the interview.

Interrogations

1. The central purpose of an interrogation is to elicit from a suspect—or from someone related to or associated with a suspect— _____ about a criminal event.

2. Before being interrogated or questioned while in police custody, an individual must be advised of his or her legal _____.

3. The *Miranda* case was actually one of _____ similar cases heard simultaneously by the Supreme Court.

4. *Miranda* warnings are intended to protect the _____ of accused people held in police custody.

5. In preparing for an interview, you should _____ all available data concerning the crime, the suspect, and the victim.

6. Because of the slightly adversarial nature of an interrogation, whenever possible it should be conducted in a setting familiar to the _____.

7. Most interrogations take place at the _____ station.

8. As in interviews, it is important to establish _____ with a suspect before beginning an interrogation.

9. Persuasion involves tapping into _____ sources of motivation: emotions, reason, and rationalization.

10. When using a logical approach, confront the suspect with convincing evidence and overwhelming _____, pointing out all of the specific elements that prove the suspect's involvement.

11. An _____ approach attempts to draw out information without specifically addressing the actual topic or subject.

12. In most jurisdictions, a juvenile's parent or guardian must be notified when the child is arrested or taken into _____.

Confessions and Admissions

1. A confession is a _____ statement in which a person charged with the commission of a _____ admits participating in or committing the criminal act in question.

2. An admission differs slightly from a _____.

3. The polygraph is a _____ device that permits an assessment of _____ associated with stress, as manifested in physiological data.

Concept Review

For each statement, write **T** *in the space provided if the entire statement is true. Write* **F** *if any part of the statement is false.*

_F_ 1. In its basic form, an interview is a therapeutic device.

_F_ 2. Interviews and interrogations are undertaken in the same manner.

_T_ 3. Interrogations are more adversarial than interviews.

_T_ 4. Rapport with the person being interviewed is a kind of empathic relationship.

_F_ 5. Interviewers generally take an adversarial attitude.

_F_ 6. The cognitive interview is one of the oldest interviewing techniques used by police in the United States.

_T_ 7. The complainant is the person seeking action by the police.

_F_ 8. If a complainant looks odd or crazy, the police need not take his or her complaint seriously.

_F_   **9.** Complaints are usually divided into three categories.

_F_   **10.** Witnesses must be advised of their constitutional rights.

_F_   **11.** Young children make especially good and reliable witnesses.

_~~F~~ T_   **12.** Before being interrogated, a suspect should be told of his or her constitutional rights.

_~~F~~ T_   **13.** Silent or disinterested witnesses may want to offer information but may be frightened.

_F_   **14.** Interrogation settings should be bright and colorful with many pictures on the walls.

_F_   **15.** The central purpose of any interrogation is to get the suspect to confess.

_T_   **16.** The logical approach is one style of interrogation.

_F_   **17.** It is never beneficial during an interrogation to under- or overstate the penalties for a crime.

_F_   **18.** Today, third-degree tactics are legal in only three states.

_~~F~~ T_   **19.** Formal interrogations generally take place at police headquarters.

_T_   **20.** Adolescents are likely to respond differently in front of their friends or parents than away from them.

Key Terms Review

Match the terms with the definitions. Write the letter of the term in the answer column.

a.	complainant	**h.**	interview
b.	interrogation	**i.**	affected words
c.	third degree	**j.**	confession
d.	polygraph	**k.**	rapport
e.	aware hearing	**l.**	alibi
f.	persuasion	**m.**	cognitive interview
g.	admission	**n.**	complaint

_H_   **1.** Questioning to obtain information regarding a person's knowledge about a crime, suspect, or event.

_B_   **2.** Questioning to obtain information from persons suspected of being directly or indirectly involved in a crime.

_K_   **3.** A relationship of mutual trust and emotional affinity that develops between an interviewer or interrogator and the person being interviewed or interrogated.

_E_   **4.** A technique of listening and really hearing what is being said, without interrupting the speaker.

_M_   **5.** An interviewing technique that helps victims or witnesses mentally put themselves at the crime scene to gather information about the crime.

_A_   **6.** An individual who seeks some satisfaction or action for an injury or for damages sustained. It may be the victim of a crime or someone who acts on behalf of the victim.

_N_ **7.** A formal allegation by which a legal action is commenced against a party; a request for police action in some matter.

_F_ **8.** Motivating and convincing a person to offer information or to comply with a request.

_I_ **9.** Words that have negative connotations in certain contexts in a given culture.

_L_ **10.** A defense offered by a suspect or defendant that attempts to prove that he or she was elsewhere when the crime in question was committed.

_C_ **11.** The use or threat of physical force, mental or emotional cruelty, or water or food deprivation to obtain a confession.

_J_ **12.** A voluntary statement—written, oral, or recorded—by an accused person, admitting participation in or commission of a criminal act.

_G_ **13.** A voluntary statement by an accused person, containing information and facts about a crime but falling short of a full confession.

_D_ **14.** A device that assesses deception by the person responding to questioning by measuring changes in various physiological data, such as respiration, depth of breathing, blood pressure, pulse, and changes in skin's electrical resistance; lie detector.

Applying Concepts

1. Using the following abbreviated facts about an armed robbery, role-play an interview with one of your classmates. Be sure to have the classmate read these facts so that he or she can more effectively act out the part of the victim.

Abbreviated Facts

The victim was taking money from his/her checking account at an automated teller machine (ATM) when a gunman came up behind him/her. The gunman demanded that the victim hand over $300 and the victim's wallet. The gunman ordered the victim to remain at the ATM and to tell no one what had happened for 10 minutes. Otherwise, he would kill the victim.

The victim, after reading these abbreviated facts, should invent appropriate answers for the questions the interviewer asks.

Questions for the Interview

_____

_____

_____

_____

_____

_____

_____

_____

_____

_____

_____

_____

_____

_____

_____

_____

2. Assume that the robber from the preceding exercise has been apprehended but the gun has not yet been found. How would you prepare to conduct an interrogation of this suspect? What sort of questions would you plan to ask? Write down a list of possible questions.

Questions

_____

_____

_____

_____

_____

_____

_____

_____

_____

_____

_____

CHAPTER 7   Fingerprints

Study Outline

Fingerprint Identification

1. Frequently, the principal evidence found at a crime scene is a _____ _____, which becomes the key to locating and identifying the perpetrator.

2. *Fingerprint* refers to any impression of the _____ ridges on a person's hands or feet.

3. It should be noted that classification of fingerprints is not identical to _____ of fingerprints.

The Nature of Fingerprints

1. Fingerprints are created by the various lines and ridges on the round area, or _____, of the end joint of every finger and thumb.

2. Generally, fingerprints are classified into three main patterns—arched, looped, and _____.

3. Ordinarily, when a suspect's fingerprints are taken, the surface of each finger is inked and the ridge patterns are transferred to a standard 8-inch by 8-inch card called a _____-_____ _____.

4. _____ _____ are impressions transferred to a surface by sweat, blood, dirt, or oil from the ridges of fingers, toes, palms, and heels.

5. Traditionally, fingerprint powders have been white or _____; today, they may also be silver, _____, or gray.

6. Rubber fingerprint lifters may also be used to recover _____.

Fingerprint Files and Searches

1. At one time all fingerprint _____ were done by hand.

2. In many ways, the process of digital fingerprinting and ink _____ are similar.

3. Today, AFIS programs are capable of making extremely fine _____ between classification points, providing considerable accuracy and reliability.

Admissibility of Fingerprint Evidence

1. The admissibility of fingerprint evidence can be traced to the case of _____ v.

_____ (1911).

2. Cases that followed the _____ decision strengthened the legitimacy of fingerprints

as a means of _____.

Concept Review

For each statement, write **T** *in the space provided if the entire statement is true. Write* **F** *if any part of the statement is false.*

T _____ 1. Fingerprints are created by friction ridges.

T _____ 2. Prints can be made by the tips of fingers, the palm of the hand, or the heel of the foot.

F _____ 3. There is no difference between classifying and identifying fingerprints.

T _____ 4. Identifying children kidnapped by family members is one use of fingerprints.

F _____ 5. Sanding the fingertips will permanently alter one's fingerprints.

F _____ 6. Generally, fingerprints are classified into four main patterns.

F _____ 7. The admissibility of fingerprints can be traced to the court case of *People v. Johnson* (1911).

T _____ 8. The plain whorl is the simplest and most common of the whorl subdivisions.

T _____ 9. Traditionally, prints have been made by inking the surface of the fingertips and transferring the ridge patterns to a ten-print card.

T _____ 10. Fingertips tend to emit a thin film of perspiration and body oil.

F _____ 11. Invisible prints can never be made visible.

T _____ 12. Plastic prints may be created in substances such as putty and butter.

T _____ 13. As a rule, all invisible prints should be photographed once developed.

T _____ 14. Magnetic brushes and powders are particularly useful for dusting plaster ceilings or slanting wooden railings.

T _____ 15. Many chemical methods have been successfully used to develop fingerprints on various surfaces.

F _____ 16. Patrol officers never use fingerprint kits.

F _____ 17. Live digital fingerprinting exists only in the movies.

F _____ 18. AFIS technology rose to national prominence in 1985, when the New York police department identified and arrested David Berkowitz, known as the Son of Sam or the 45-Caliber Killer.

Key Terms Review

Match the terms with the definitions. Write the letter of the term in the answer column.

a. invisible print
b. dactylography
c. fingerprint
d. ten-print card
e. classification
f. elimination prints
g. latent print

h. friction ridges
i. plastic print
j. identification
k. bulb
l. visible print
m. automated fingerprint identification system

_C_ **1.** An impression created by friction ridges on a person's hands and feet.

_H_ **2.** Minute, raised lines on the surface of fingertips, palms, toes, and heels.

_E_ **3.** A method of organizing fingerprints.

_J_ **4.** The determination of an individual's identity through physical evidence, especially fingerprint evidence.

_B_ **5.** The scientific study of fingerprints as a means of identification.

_K_ **6.** The rounded area at the end joint of every finger and thumb.

_D_ **7.** A card or form on which fingerprints are recorded, along with other personal data, and then filed for future retrieval.

_G_ **8.** An impression transferred to a surface by sweat, oil, dirt, blood, or some other substance on the ridges of the fingers; it may be visible or invisible.

_L_ **9.** A fingerprint, found at a crime scene, that is immediately visible to the naked eye.

_A_ **10.** A latent print not visible without some form of developing.

_I_ **11.** A type of visible print formed when substances such as butter, grease, wax, peanut butter, and so forth that have a plastic-like texture are touched.

_F_ **12.** Fingerprints taken of all persons whose prints are likely to be found at a crime scene, but who have a lawful reason to have been there and are not suspects.

_m_ **13.** A computerized system for scanning, mapping, storing, searching, and retrieving fingerprints.

Applying Concepts

1. You are a patrol officer in a small police department. You have been asked to put together a fingerprint kit for as little cost as possible. What will you include in this kit?

_____

_____

_____

_____

_____

_____

_____

_____

_____

_____

_____

2. Using an ink pad or a piece of paper on which you have scribbled with a lead pencil, make a print of your right thumb below. After cleaning up, examine this print, and identify the core and any deltas, whorls, arches, and loops.

CHAPTER 8   From Surveillance to Records and Files

Study Outline

Observing the Scene

1. Surveillance is the _____ of people, groups, places, vehicles, and things over a long period.

2. Unlike other parts of police work, for which the officer can prepare and plan, surveillance depends largely on the _____ of the subject.

3. There are no hard-and-fast _____ governing surveillance.

4. In general, surveillance is used to obtain _____ about people, their friends and associates, and _____ that may assist in solving a criminal case.

5. Before beginning a surveillance, you should become _____ with all the available facts of the case and the purpose of the surveillance.

Types of Surveillance

1. Fixed, or _____, surveillance uses a single location, from which the surveillants operate and observe the target, or subject, of the surveillance.

2. To establish a fixed surveillance, the primary requirement is good _____ of the subject or location being watched.

3. Three-investigator surveillance is sometimes referred to as _____ surveillance.

4. Before a vehicle surveillance is begun, the _____ equipment should be checked to make sure it is in good working order.

5. The use of planes and helicopters for _____ surveillance is becoming more common.

6. Current provisions for using electronic listening devices can be traced to the landmark case of _____ v. _____ (1967).

Tips for Surveillance Operations

1. Officers on surveillance should try to _____ in with other people and activities in the area.

2. During any surveillance, the officer must be both stealthful and _____.

3. The surveillant should never immediately conclude that he or she has been _____ (identified as an officer).

Records and Files

1. The more sources an investigator is comfortable using, the easier _____ become.

2. There are a number of obvious _____ that contain information about people.

3. Utilities often require _____ from customers who have never had a utility account.

4. Today it is virtually impossible to live and work in society without taking part in many _____ transactions.

Concept Review

For each statement, write **T** *in the space provided if the entire statement is true. Write* **F** *if any part of the statement is false.*

_F_ 1. *Surveillance* can be defined as special operations with the tactical team.

_F_ 2. Surveillance must be spontaneous and undertaken without planning.

_F_ 3. Wiretaps can be used whenever an officer has a reasonable suspicion that a suspect is involved in a crime.

_T_ 4. In general, surveillance is used to gather information.

_T_ 5. Before beginning a surveillance, participating officers should become familiar with all the facts in the case.

_T_ 6. The two broadest areas of surveillance can be categorized as fixed and moving surveillance.

_T_ 7. Fixed surveillance and stationary surveillance are the same kind of activity.

_T_ 8. Moving surveillance is more complex and difficult than fixed surveillance.

_F_ 9. Surveillance can never be undertaken by a single officer.

_T_ 10. Three-investigator surveillance is sometimes called ABC surveillance.

_F_ 11. Three-investigator surveillance is sometimes called perimeter box surveillance.

_T_ 12. Before beginning a vehicular surveillance, officers should check their communications equipment.

_T_ 13. Officers on surveillance often wear disguises.

_F_ 14. When confronted by a suspect, the officer is legally required to admit that he or she is following the suspect.

_F_ 15. Stakeouts are undertaken only to locate fugitives.

_T_ 16. The use of various audio devices is limited by legal restrictions.

_F_ 17. Wiretaps are illegal in seven states.

_T_ **18.** Investigators make use of many files and records held outside the police department.

_T_ **19.** In some cases, officers may locate a suspect simply by asking members of his or her family.

_T_ **20.** When someone applies for utilities, he or she may create a paper trail.

Key Terms Review

Match the terms with the definitions. Write the letter of the term in the answer column.

a. perimeter box surveillance
b. moving surveillance
c. surveillance
d. criminal jackets
e. leading surveillance

f. convoy
g. ABC surveillance
h. fixed, or stationary, surveillance
i. one-consenting-party rule
j. close surveillance

_C_ **1.** The secret observation of people, groups, places, vehicles, and things over a prolonged period to gather information about a crime or criminal.

_h_ **2.** Close watch on a subject or object from a single location, such as a building or vehicle.

_B_ **3.** The observation of a subject while moving on foot, in a vehicle, or in an aircraft.

_g_ **4.** A three-officer foot surveillance in which Officer A follows the suspect and in turn is followed by Officer B. The third surveillant, Officer C, normally walks on the other side of the street, opposite the suspect.

_e_ **5.** The procedure of watching and following a subject while remaining ahead of the subject.

_j_ **6.** Surveillance conducted while remaining very close to the subject.

_A_ **7.** A vehicle surveillance technique that allows surveillants to maintain coverage even if the subject suddenly turns at an intersection.

_i_ **8.** A legal principle that permits the audio recording of a two-party conversation if one party has consented.

_f_ **9.** The following of a subject by multiple individuals.

_d_ **10.** Official police records of criminals.

Applying Concepts

1. What are some important legal factors an investigator must consider before starting a wiretap on a suspect?

_____

_____

_____

_____

_____

_____

_____

_____

2. You are working for a police department. You have been given the job of locating a man known as Charles Agnew. His last known address was 136 Maple Street, where he lived with a cousin for five years. He has apparently skipped town. What sources of information might you consider in your effort to trace his current location?

_____

_____

_____

_____

_____

_____

_____

_____

_____

_____

_____

_____

_____

CHAPTER 9   Writing Reports

Study Outline

Communicating Through Reports

1. _____ communication is essential in all police work, and criminal investigation is no exception.

2. Police reports must set forth information in an accurate, _____, clear, and complete manner.

3. Reports provide information to fellow _____ working on a case, to supervisors and administrators who may need to allocate resources for a case, and to the _____ attorney who may try the case.

4. The six basic questions on which an officer can hang the facts of a case are the following:

   a. _____

   b. _____

   c. _____

   d. _____

   e. _____

   f. _____

5. One could easily compile a lengthy checklist of _____ of a solid report.

6. The three basic tests of a good report are as follows:

   a. _____

   _____

   b. _____

   _____

   c. _____

   _____

7. Reports provide the _____ needed to investigate and apprehend criminals and to solve crimes.

Characteristics of a Good Report

1. A report may contain all the necessary information, but if it is _____ written, these points may be lost.

2. Completeness means that the report contains all pertinent _____.

3. It is a good evaluation technique to have fellow officers _____ your report.

4. A report must exhibit clarity; that is, it must _____ explain to a reader exactly what the officer saw, heard, and _____.

5. Reports must demonstrate accuracy to be _____.

6. Conscientious efforts must be made to avoid sexist _____.

7. Be aware that some cultures frequently place the _____ name first and the given name second.

8. When property is taken, a complete and _____ description may assist in its recovery.

9. All pertinent information about an area should be included in a description entered in the _____ report.

10. Differences in reporting forms are the result of department needs, requirements, policies, and _____.

Types of Reports

1. Police agencies tend to use five basic categories of forms and reports:

   a. _____

   b. _____

   c. _____

   d. _____

   e. _____

2. Misdemeanor reports record all _____ crimes and miscellaneous incidents.

3. Sometimes, after completing a misdemeanor or miscellaneous report, an investigator may determine that the incident was actually a _____, an attempted felony, or a crime that requires a felony report.

4. The information required in a felony report is much more detailed than that required in a

_____ report.

5. To the extent possible, each crime report should describe only _____ offense.

6. A follow-up report, sometimes called a _____ report, is made after the initial report.

7. An arrest report documents the circumstances of the _____ or detention of individuals by the police.

8. An arrest report, like most other reports, has a form section and a _____ section.

The Completed Report

1. When a written report is _____, it is reviewed by the officer's immediate supervisor.

2. Police reports carry _____ needed for making a wide variety of important decisions about the liberty of a suspect in a crime or the role of parties involved in an incident.

Concept Review

For each statement, write **T** *in the space provided if the entire statement is true. Write* **F** *if any part of the statement is false.*

___F___ 1. Copspeak was developed to use in official reports.

___T___ 2. Accuracy and clarity are two important qualities in police reports.

___T___ 3. Even very minor mistakes in police reports can damage a prosecution.

___T___ 4. Obtaining correct information about addresses and types of buildings is important in report writing.

___F___ 5. It is not worthwhile to consider why a suspect chose a particular victim over another.

___F___ 6. All police agencies require a one-paragraph synopsis at the beginning of every crime report.

___T___ 7. Reports permit police accountability both inside and outside the agency.

___F___ 8. Reports are seldom read by anyone other than the officer who wrote them, and his or her immediate supervisor.

___F___ 9. Police reports need only be approximately accurate.

___T___ 10. It is a good idea to have a fellow officer read one's report before turning it in.

___T___ 11. Profanity should not be used in police reports.

_T_ **12.** One reason the structure and content of basic police reports vary is the diversity of the needs of various departments.

_F_ **13.** The information required in the form section of a police report generally does not include the case file number.

_T_ **14.** Regardless of other differences, felony reports tend to be a little longer than misdemeanor reports in most jurisdictions.

_T_ **15.** The narrative portion of a felony report should be as brief as possible, avoiding all unnecessary verbiage.

_T_ **16.** Whenever possible, each crime report should describe only one offense.

_F_ **17.** Follow-up reports are sometimes called "ancillary reports."

_T_ **18.** An arrest report documents the circumstances of an arrest or detention.

_T_ **19.** In a traffic fatality, the vehicle accident report will become part of the homicide investigation.

_F_ **20.** The district attorney is the only person outside the police department who ever reads the police report.

Key Terms Review

Match the terms with the definitions. Write the letter of the term in the answer column.

a. synopsis
b. vehicle accident report
c. cop speak
d. evidence report
e. form section
f. arrest report

g. narrative section
h. felony report
i. follow-up, or supplementary, report
j. property report
k. complaint, or incident, report
l. sexist language

_C_ **1.** Specialized vocabulary, or jargon, used by police.

_L_ **2.** Insensitive, politically incorrect language used in reference to gender or gender issues.

_e_ **3.** A boxed section of a police report form designed for fill-in and check-off of information.

_g_ **4.** A lined or blank section of a police report form, designed for detailed descriptions and accounts of events.

_A_ **5.** A summary or abstract of a larger body of writing, such as a police report.

_K_ **6.** A police report written to document events surrounding misdemeanor crimes and incidents of a miscellaneous nature.

_h_ **7.** A police record created to document the events surrounding a felony.

_j_ **8.** A report directed toward documenting property taken or damaged in a crime.

_d_ **9.** A report written about the evidence found at a crime scene; usually an evidence inventory is attached as part of the report.

_i_ **10.** A report written during the secondary stage of a criminal investigation.

_F_ **11.** A police record created to document the events surrounding an arrest.

_B_ **12.** A police record created to document the events surrounding a vehicular accident.

Applying Concepts

The following unacceptable report concerns a hypothetical robbery of the proprietor of the Motel 6 in Withville, Virginia, on August 13, 1998. The report contains many unnecessary words and sentences and is poorly written. You are to rewrite the report, correcting all errors. Use good sentence structure and punctuation and proper paragraph arrangement.

Robbery at the Motel 6

Facts

It was an unseasonably cold and rainy day, although it is given to rain quite a bit in August. It was August, 13, 1998 at 1130 hours, the proprietor of the Motel 6 at Withville, Virginia, Mr. John A Fisher, was preparing to leave form his living quarters at the motel for an extended vacation in Florida. He was planning to make the trip in his new Dodge Ram pickup truck, with a club cab, bright red in color, a really nice truck. This was the first truck Mister Fisher had ever owned, having traded in a Toyota Tercel, which he did not think he was given sufficient trade-in value for. The Motel 6 is a franchise, but Mister Fisher and his brother Morris helped with the architectural plans for its construction. Mr. heard a knock at the door to his apartment, number 8 at the motel, and when he opened it and unknown white man rushed inside the room and pointed a blue steel revolver toward Mr. Fisher's head and ordered him to open the wall safe located behind a print of an oil painting of the blue ridge mountains at sunset given to Mr. Fisher by his mother before she died several years ago. Mr. Fisher told me that the bandit told him": Hurry up I've been watching you for days, I have nothing to lose if I kill you." Mister Fisher stated he opened his safe and gave the bandit all the contents which he told me included $2500, one man's white gold ring with the initials JAF on the onyx setting valued at one hundred and fifty dollars, and one string of pearls valued as $800.00. The pearls were an heirloom and handed down to Mr. Fisher by his Grandmother Nellie Fisher who lived to be 101. but sadly died several years ago. He was planning to give the pearls to his only niece, Miss Helen Fisher for a wedding gift. Helen is engaged to marry her childhood sweetheart, Thomas Katz, on September 7, 1998. The robbery loss totaled $3450 plus the $185 the robber got from a small cigar box located beneath the reception counter. Mr. Fisher felt quite elated over the fact that he was fully covered by insurance which he had obtained only a month previous to this robbery. The bandit placed the loot in his topcoat pocket and ordered Mister Fisher to face the wall and stay there for ten minutes or, "I'll blow your damned head off." "I'll be watching you." Mr. Fisher stated the bandit then left by the same door he had entered from, and two minutes later Mr. Fisher heard a car speed away from the parking lot. Not knowing of this was the robber's car, he waited for about three more minutes, then telephoned the police department and reported the robbery. When I arrived, Mr. Fisher described the bandit as follows: 5'5" to 5'7", 165–175 pounds, stocky build, about twenty-eight to thirty years-old, ruddy complexion, sandy blond hair and blue eyes, wearing an olive green baseball cap, a black oilcloth duster, dark black cowboy boots with a red S-shaped design on the side, and black leather driving gloves. Mr. Fisher stated the bandit held the pistol in his right hand. It was Mister Fisher's opinion that the bandit was probably driving a new car because of his neat appearance, but he had not seen what car the bandit drove away in. Other than Mr. Fisher, no one could be found at the motel who had heard or seen anything. We decided contact the dispatcher and broadcast the bandit's description. After that, we asked Mr. Fisher to accompany us to the police headquarters to observe our mug file for possible suspects. He was unable to make any identification.

The investigation will continue.

_____

_____

_____

_____

_____

_____

_____

_____

_____

_____

_____

_____

_____

_____

_____

_____

_____

_____

_____

_____

Name _____ Date _____

_____

_____

_____

_____

_____

_____

_____

_____

_____

_____

_____

_____

_____

_____

_____

_____

_____

_____

_____

_____

_____

_____

_____

_____

_____

_____

_____

CHAPTER 10   Robbery

Study Outline

Overview of Robbery

1. Television and movies have created an image of robbers from yesteryear as _____ and

_____ characters.

2. Robbery is among the _____ criminal problems facing law enforcement officers in America today.

3. Robbery does not always involve only the loss of money or _____.

4. The UCR for 1995 indicated that firearms were used in 41 percent of _____, strong-arm tactics in another 41 percent, knives or cutting instruments in 9 percent, and other

_____ in the remainder.

Legal Elements of Robbery

1. Robbery is the unlawful _____ or attempted taking of another's personal property in his

or her immediate possession and against his or her will by _____ or threat of force.

2. State statutes precisely _____ the crime of robbery.

Categories of Robbery

1. Robberies can be divided into four categories according to the *modus operandi* of the perpetrator:

a. _____

b. _____

c. _____

d. _____

2. Residential robberies are less frequent than other types of robberies. In 1995, they represented about

_____ percent of all robberies in the UCR.

3. Home invaders are terroristic, using _____ or threats of violence to intimidate the victim into submission.

4. In a street robbery, the _____ may be injured when pushed to the ground or when struck as the robber flees.

5. Taxicabs are a likely target because they can easily be lured to a location with a simple _____ call.

6. In the early 1980s, the news media began reporting stories about a category of violent _____ called carjacking.

7. Carjackers use surprise and _____ to carry out their robberies.

Classification of Robbers

1. Robbers can be divided into four groups according to motive and general worldview:

   a. _____

   b. _____

   c. _____

   d. _____

2. Professional robbers have incorporated robbery into their _____ and have committed themselves to this crime form as a means of economic support.

3. Drug-addicted robbers typically rob to support a _____ habit.

Investigation of Robberies

1. Robbery has a comparatively low rate of clearance by _____.

2. When the police are informed of a robbery, the robber has usually _____.

3. An officer arriving on the scene of a robbery has three primary objectives:

   a. _____

   b. _____

   c. _____

4. Action stereotyping occurs when an officer misreads common or stereotypic _____ of people at or near a crime scene.

5. The _____ officer to arrive at the crime scene should conduct brief interviews with all parties concerned.

6. Often robberies leave little physical _____ for the police to use.

7. Hidden _____ cameras have been used successfully in banks, large department stores, and even small convenience stores.

Concept Review

For each statement, write **T** *in the space provided if the entire statement is true. Write* **F** *if any part of the statement is false.*

___F___ 1. Robbery is not a very serious crime in America today.

___F___ 2. Guns and other weapons are seldom used in robberies.

___T___ 3. Both fear and force are necessary for a crime to be classified as a robbery.

___F___ 4. A robbery of a hotel room would not be a residential burglary, since no one really lives there.

___F___ 5. Street robberies are the easiest type of robbery to solve.

___T___ 6. Home invaders sometimes work in a specific ethnic community.

___T___ 7. Usually, armored car robberies are undertaken by professionals.

___T___ 8. Professional robbers tend to see robbery as their job.

___T___ 9. Opportunistic robbers typically steal small amounts of money whenever a likely target presents itself.

___F___ 10. Addicts typically rob to acquire money for food.

___T___ 11. Usually, by the time the police are notified about a robbery, it is over.

___T___ 12. When police do hear about a robbery in progress, time is a critical factor.

___F___ 13. Situational stereotypes seldom create serious problems for police officers.

___T___ 14. The order of investigative activities in robbery cases is dictated by the facts of each situation.

___T___ 15. To expedite the gathering of information from witnesses at robbery crime scenes, some agencies use a standardized form to record witness data.

Key Terms Review

Match the terms with the definitions. Write the letter of the term in the answer column.

a. situational stereotyping
b. professional robber
c. residential robbery
d. clear
e. crime index
f. alcoholic robber
g. street robbery
h. action stereotyping

i. opportunistic robber
j. commercial robbery
k. carjacking
l. physical stereotyping
m. index offense
n. drug-addicted robber
o. vehicle-driver robbery
p. robbery

___E___ 1. A collection of statistics in the FBI's Uniform Crime Reports on the numbers of murder, rape, robbery, assault, burglary, larceny-theft, motor vehicle theft, and arson crimes reported in a calendar year.

___M___ 2. One of the eight crimes (murder, rape, assault, robbery, burglary, larceny-theft, motor vehicle theft, and arson) that the FBI considers the most serious, which are combined to create the crime index.

___D___ 3. To solve a criminal case by arresting at least one person, charging him or her with the crime, and turning him or her over to the courts for prosecution.

___P___ 4. The unlawful taking or attempted taking of another's personal property in his or her immediate possession and against his or her will by force or the threat of force.

___C___ 5. A robbery in which the target is a private residence, a hotel or motel room, a trailer or mobile home, or other attached areas of a residence.

___J___ 6. The robbery of a commercial location such as a bank, service station, restaurant, or convenience store.

___G___ 7. Any of an assortment of robberies that occur in street settings.

___O___ 8. Robbery of an object of value in or attached to a vehicle or from the driver of the vehicle.

___K___ 9. Robbery of a car with the driver and/or occupants still inside it.

___B___ 10. A person who has incorporated robbery into a lifestyle and robs as a means of economic support.

___I___ 11. A person who steals small amounts of property or cash whenever the opportunity presents itself.

___N___ 12. A person who robs to sustain an addiction to some type of illegal drug.

___F___ 13. A person who robs to sustain an addiction to alcohol or who attributes criminal action to the influence of alcohol.

___H___ 14. Misreading common or stereotypic behaviors of people at or near a crime scene who may actually be the offenders.

___L___ 15. A misconception that suggests that a criminal is a certain type of person.

___A___ 16. False or mistaken conclusions about the appearance of certain situations.

Applying Concepts

1. You and your partner have just responded to a robbery call at a crowded supermarket. While conducting an immediate investigation, you are suddenly confronted by a robbery suspect, a man who has surprised and disarmed your partner. The suspect loudly demands that you drop your gun and threatens to kill your partner. Confronted with this extremely serious situation, how would you react? Explain your answer.

_____

_____

_____

_____

_____

_____

_____

_____

_____

_____

_____

_____

_____

_____

_____

_____

_____

_____

_____

_____

Criminal Investigation—Study Guide **55**

2. At 1200 hours, you are off duty and unarmed, and you are about to enter a drugstore to have a prescription filled. Suddenly, you notice that four of the customers in the store have their hands up in the air. You also notice two men, each holding a revolver. The robbers do not see you. What action will you take? Explain your answer.

_____

_____

_____

_____

_____

_____

_____

_____

_____

_____

_____

_____

_____

_____

_____

_____

_____

_____

_____

_____

_____

_____

CHAPTER 11   Assault

Study Outline

Overview of Assault

1. An assault is an unlawful attempt or threat to commit a _____ injury to another by the use of force.

2. In 1995, firearms were the _____ of choice in 22.9 percent of all aggravated assaults, knives or cutting instruments in 18.3 percent, and personal weapons in 25.9 percent.

Legal Elements of the Crime of Assault

1. At one time, in many states, the term *assault* referred to threats or attempts to cause bodily

   _____.

2. The term _____ referred to the actual carrying out of these threats of physical harm.

3. Simple assault is usually a _____.

4. Aggravated assaults are usually committed with a weapon that is likely to produce a

   _____ injury or a potentially fatal wound.

5. Stalking is behavior in which a person "intentionally and repeatedly _____, attempts to contact, harasses, and/or intimidates another person."

Investigating Assaults

1. In many assault cases, the assailant and the victim _____ each other well or are at least acquainted with one another.

2. The relationship between parties in an assault can create certain investigative _____.

3. When investigating an aggravated _____, investigators must be sure to obtain all facts relating to the complaint.

Domestic Assault

1. Intrafamily _____, as many sociologists now call the phenomenon, has become a

   serious and perplexing problem in the United States in recent _____.

2. In a study published in 1977, the police foundation examined domestic _____ and domestic homicides that occurred in Kansas City, Missouri, during a two-year period.

3. It is important that officers consider carefully whether they should or should not make an _____ on a domestic assault call.

4. In New York, only weeks after the murder of Nicole Simpson, the state legislature unanimously passed a sweeping bill that mandates arrest for any person who commits a _____ assault.

5. It has been estimated that _____ million women and men are battered by spouses each year.

6. Child abuse can be physical harm, including sexual _____, as well as emotional harm.

7. The clinical term for injuries suffered by physically abused children is _____ child syndrome.

8. Elder family members may also be the object of _____ violence.

Concept Review

*For each statement, write **T** in the space provided if the entire statement is true. Write **F** if any part of the statement is false.*

___F___ 1. In 1995, firearms were used in assaults more than any other weapon.

___T___ 2. The term *battery* once referred to the actual carrying out of a threat to do physical harm.

___F___ 3. Simple assault does not require the ability to do bodily harm.

___T___ 4. Aggravated assaults are usually committed with some form of weapon.

___F___ 5. There are no formal laws against stalking.

___T___ 6. In most assault cases, the assailant is well known to the victim, or they are at least acquainted.

___T___ 7. The relationships of parties involved in a domestic assault may create certain investigative problems.

___F___ 8. *Complacency* means being very alert and attentive to what is going on around you.

___F___ 9. Many sociologists call violence between family members *dysfunctional violence-effect*.

___T___ 10. Some research suggests that it is better to make an arrest in domestic disputes than merely to talk to both parties.

___T___ 11. Many jurisdictions have developed domestic violence acts that require officers to make arrests if evidence of violence is present.

___F___ 12. Child abuse involves only physical harm to a child.

___T___ 13. The tendency to abuse children is sometimes increased by such problems as unemployment and low self-esteem.

_____ **14.** Munchausen Syndrome is named after a fabulous liar.

_____ **15.** Typically, it is a health professional who brings to the attention of authorities a case of Munchausen Syndrome by Proxy.

Key Terms Review

Match the terms with the definitions. Write the letter of the term in the answer column.

a.	intrafamily violence	**h.**	simple assault
b.	restraining order	**i.**	complacency
c.	child abuse	**j.**	domestic violence statute
d.	battery	**k.**	stalking
e.	domestic assault	**l.**	citizen's arrest
f.	aggravated (felonious) assault	**m.**	assault
g.	battered child syndrome		

_____ **1.** An unlawful attempt or threat to commit a physical injury to another through use of force.

_____ **2.** Once, the actual carrying out of the threat of physical harm in an assault; today, in most jurisdictions, the term is synonymous with *assault.*

_____ **3.** The intentional causing of fear in a person of immediate bodily harm or death.

_____ **4.** An unlawful attack on another person with the intention of causing severe bodily harm.

_____ **5.** Intentionally and repeatedly following, attempting to contact, harassing, or intimidating another person.

_____ **6.** Court order requiring a person to do or refrain from doing a particular thing.

_____ **7.** Any type of battery that occurs between individuals who are related or between individuals and their significant others.

_____ **8.** Unconcern resulting from having grown accustomed to a given pattern of events or behavior.

_____ **9.** An arrest by a private citizen, as contrasted with a police officer, permitted under certain circumstances, generally for a felony or for a misdemeanor amounting to a breach of the peace.

_____ **10.** Any type of violent behavior that occurs within a family.

_____ **11.** A state law that outlaws physical violence against any family member; responding officers serve as the complainant in domestic situations under certain circumstances.

_____ **12.** Physical harm, including sexual abuse, or emotional harm to children.

_____ **13.** The group of injuries suffered by physically abused children.

Applying Concepts

1. For each of the following descriptions, determine whether the event is a simple assault, an aggravated assault, or no assault at all.

   a. A five-year-old boy accidentally hits another five-year-old boy with his Tonka truck.

   _____

   b. Mrs. Richey slaps her son's teacher after the teacher accuses the boy of cheating on a test.

   _____

   c. John punches Bill at a bar after they disagree over a football score.

   _____

   d. Janet breaks a pool cue over Thomas's head because he admits to dating other women.

   _____

   e. Jack spills hot coffee on his boss because he wasn't given a raise—but Jack pretends it was an accident. Ted knows the truth, because Jack told him his plan.

   _____

   f. Officer McSkimming hits a violent and resisting suspect with his baton while making a lawful arrest.

   _____

2. For each of the foregoing situations, explain why it is a simple assault, an aggravated assault, or no assault.

   a. _____

   _____

   _____

   _____

   _____

   _____

   _____

   _____

   _____

   _____

b. _____

_____

_____

_____

_____

_____

_____

_____

c. _____

_____

_____

_____

_____

_____

_____

_____

d. _____

_____

_____

_____

_____

e.

f.

CHAPTER 12   Sexual Assault and Rape

Study Outline

Overview of Sex Crimes

1. Sex crimes represent a broad classification of illegal _____.

2. Forcible rape is the only sex offense that is an _____ crime.

Classification of Sex Crimes

1. The term *sex crime* covers a multitude of _____, ranging from indecent exposure to forcible rape.

2. Even when there is mutual consent, there are a number of acts that remain _____.

Legal Elements of the Crime of Rape

1. Rape is usually classified as either _____ or statutory.

2. Statutory rape is sexual intercourse with a _____.

3. The basic *corpus delicti* in most forcible rape statutes includes these three elements:

   a. _____

   b. _____

   c. _____

4. Many victims develop an overwhelming feeling of _____, shame, and worthlessness after a sexual assault.

Investigating Sex Offenses

1. An appropriate, understanding, and sensitive _____ is essential in sexual assault cases.

2. During the past decade, many police departments have developed rape _____, which are usually kept in the emergency rooms of local hospitals.

3. Preliminary interviews with victims should seek information about the _____, the location where the assault occurred, and any relevant circumstances surrounding the offense.

1. Child molesting is a broad _____ that includes any behavior motivated by an unusual or abnormal sexual interest in _____.

2. The crime of indecent exposure is among the most _____ of the standard sex offenses.

3. The _____ surrounding the offense of incest vary from state to state.

4. Pedophiles, or adults who are sexually attracted to _____, prey on the vulnerability of children.

5. Like rape, child molestation is not primarily motivated by _____ gratification.

6. A number of federal and state regulations require teachers, doctors, and child care workers to _____ to police any suspicion of child abuse.

7. Children who have been severely brutalized may not be able to provide _____ information.

8. _____ dolls are dolls with gender-appropriate genitalia.

9. A problem investigators face when interviewing child victims is that young children have very short _____ spans.

Concept Review

For each statement, write **T** *in the space provided if the entire statement is true. Write* **F** *if any part of the statement is false.*

_____ 1. Sex crimes represent a narrow and limited set of criminal behaviors.

_____ 2. Forcible rape and child molestation are the only two sex crimes considered index crimes.

_____ 3. Rape is considered the least reported of the index crimes.

_____ 4. Prostitution is not illegal if both parties have mutually consented to the sex act.

_____ 5. Rape is usually classified as either forcible or statutory.

_____ 6. The nationally recognized definition of a minor is a female under the age of 18.

_____ 7. Some states have substituted the words *sexual assault* for the word *rape* in their statutes.

_____ 8. Officers need not worry about victims' feelings during interviews when they are trying to catch a brutal rapist.

_____ 9. A slang term prison inmates use for child molesters is "short-eyes."

_____ 10. Indecent exposure is among the most common of the standard sex offenses.

_____ 11. Incest is a universal taboo, with identical statutes in all states in America.

_____ 12. Another term for a child molester is *pedophile.*

_____ 13. The majority of pedophiles are under age 35 at the time of their first arrest.

_____ 14. According to some research studies, many child molesters are married.

_____ 15. Child molestation is motivated primarily by sexual gratification.

_____ 16. In many states, laws require teachers, doctors, and child care workers to report to authorities any suspicions they have of child abuse.

_____ 17. Most police departments across the nation do not have personnel with the special training and skill needed to investigate child molestation cases.

_____ 18. Multidisciplinary teams do not provide much additional advantage over traditional police investigations.

_____ 19. Investigators should have some understanding of child development.

_____ 20. Some child molestation investigations require officers to show victims dolls.

Key Terms Review

Match the terms with the definitions. Write the letter of the term in the answer column.

a. date rape
b. sex crime
c. sexual seduction
d. incest
e. forcible rape
f. indecent exposure
g. mutual consent
h. contributing to the delinquency
   of a minor

i. statutory rape
j. lewd and lascivious behavior
   with a child
k. rape
l. child molesting
m. anatomical dolls
n. rape kit
o. pedophile

_____ 1. Any of an assortment of criminal violations related to sexual conduct.

_____ 2. Willing participation by both parties in sexual acts.

_____ 3. Sexual intercourse against a person's will by the use or threat of force.

_____ 4. Sexual intercourse with a minor, with or without the minor's consent.

_____ 5. An act of sexual intercourse, or penetration of the victim's vagina, without consent from the victim, and against the victim's will by force, coercion, or duress.

_____ 6. Forced sexual intercourse that occurs between friends or acquaintances or while a couple is on a date; also called *acquaintance rape*.

_____ 7. An evidence kit used in many hospital emergency rooms to secure physical evidence specimens in rape cases.

_____ 8. A broad term encompassing any behavior motivated by an unnatural sexual interest in minor children.

_____ 9. Sexual intercourse between an adult and a willing minor.

_____ 10. Touching any part of a child to arousal; appealing to or gratifying the sexual desires of either the child or the perpetrating adult.

_____ 11. Exhibiting the private parts of one's body in a lewd or indecent manner to the sight of others in a public place.

_____ 12. An act of omission that contributes to or tends to make a child delinquent.

_____ 13. Sexual intercourse between persons who are so closely related that their marriage is illegal or forbidden by custom.

_____ 14. An adult who is sexually attracted to children or performs sexual acts with children.

_____ 15. Dolls or puppets with sex-appropriate genitalia, used in interviews with suspected child victims of sexual abuse or assault.

Applying Concepts

The following case facts present a grave problem that you, as the investigator, must confront. After carefully reviewing the facts, write a short statement describing and explaining the decision you would make under these circumstances.

Facts of the Case

A 15-year-old girl was abducted while walking home from school on Tuesday afternoon. She is the daughter of good, responsible parents of ordinary circumstances. Investigation discloses that she was picked up by a man named HENDERSON and taken to Rachel's, a local house of prostitution. There she was given to JANET COLLDER, the house madam, as payment for a debt HENDERSON owed her.

The girl remained at the house of prostitution for three days. During that time, the madam of the house said, the girl appeared drugged, seemed ill, and did not eat any food. Finally, COLLDER became nervous, contacted HENDERSON, and ordered him to take the girl out of the house. COLLDER had become afraid because of both the girl's age and her health.

Several days later, HENDERSON was apprehended at a bar in town and transported to the town jail. You are one of two vice officers assigned to the case. You and your partner interrogate HENDERSON, trying to determine the facts of the case and the location of the girl. Although HENDERSON waives his *Miranda* rights, he refuses to admit any knowledge of the girl or her whereabouts. When confronted with the statement by COLLDER that he had brought the girl to her, he flatly denies it and calls COLLDER a "filthy whore liar."

It seems clear that HENDERSON is lying; yet you have now exhausted all legal approaches to interrogation. These methods have failed to obtain any information about the missing girl. You and your partner are convinced he knows exactly where the girl is. You are further convinced that time is of the greatest importance and that the girl's life is in danger. You are certain that if this man tells you what he knows you can save the life of an innocent child. You must get information from this suspect—or release him. What will you do?

_____

_____

_____

_____

_____

_____

_____

_____

CHAPTER 13   Kidnapping and Extortion

Study Outline

Kidnapping

1. Kidnapping is taking someone away by _____, often for ransom, or some form of payment.

2. In many recent kidnappings, the _____ have been relatives of the kidnappers.

3. Terrorists have for years used kidnapping to coerce governments into changing policies or releasing

    _____.

4. Federal kidnapping legislation was a response to a series of kidnappings for ransom in the

    _____ and 1930s.

5. The most notorious of these seizures was the kidnapping and murder of the son of Charles

    _____, a hero because of his trans-Atlantic flight.

6. The federal kidnapping statute, sometimes referred to as the _____ law, was
    passed on June 22, 1932.

7. Alleged kidnappings may actually be attempts to _____ up murders.

8. It is important to obtain the exact _____ of the ransom note, letter, or telephone call.

Hostage Taking

1. Hostage takers are usually _____ whose escape from a crime scene has been inter-
    rupted, either by the police or by another individual.

2. Many of the larger municipal police departments, the FBI, and a number of other federal agencies now

    have _____ negotiators ready to deal with cases involving hostages.

3. When people are taken as hostages, the last thing their captors want is to have to _____ them.

4. There are three general principles to follow in hostage or kidnapping situations:

    a. _____

    b. _____

    c. _____

5. Mentally unbalanced or psychotic hostage takers are usually looking for a forum to make a statement

or to get some _____ out.

Child Stealing

1. Recently, a new form of kidnapping has become prominent. This offense is committed against the

_____ or other legal guardian and not against the child.

2. To be classified as child stealing, the taking of a _____ must only be against the will or without the consent of the parent, guardian, or person with legal custody.

Extortion

1. Extortion is the _____ of money, property, or other consideration by one party from another with the appearance of consent.

2. To constitute extortion, the wrongful use of force or fear must produce _____.

3. In some jurisdictions, extortion is simply referred to as _____.

4. Extortionists deliver their threats by various means, including telephone, electronic computer communications networks or bulletin boards, and _____.

5. Often, solving an extortion case requires the complete cooperation of the _____.

6. In many respects, extortion investigations are similar to _____ investigations.

Concept Review

*For each statement, write **T** in the space provided if the entire statement is true. Write **F** if any part of the statement is false.*

_____ **1.** Kidnapping is defined as the theft of kids.

_____ **2.** Kidnappers are usually motivated by a mental imbalance.

_____ **3.** Of the crimes that confront police officers, kidnappings are among the easiest to solve.

_____ **4.** In kidnapping cases in which the fate of the victim is uncertain, the media tend to show considerable attention.

_____ **5.** The Lindbergh child was 24 months old when he was abducted in 1932.

_____ **6.** The Federal Kidnapping Act of 1932 is also known as the Augustus Act, after the son of Lindbergh, Charles Augustus Lindbergh.

_____ **7.** There is a tendency among some people to label all disappearances kidnappings.

_____ **8.** Disappearances may involve youngsters who have simply run away from home.

_____ 9. The immediate concern of law enforcement during any kidnapping is the life and safe return of the victim.

_____ 10. All activities around the kidnapping victim's home should be kept at a low profile.

_____ 11. When reporters learn about a kidnapping, the police are required by law to offer full disclosure of all information.

_____ 12. The secondary stage of a kidnapping investigation is generally the period after the victim has been returned or the victim's body has been discovered.

_____ 13. Certain confidential information about the kidnapping should be withheld from the media.

_____ 14. When necessary, it is important to lie to hostage takers.

_____ 15. One of the most important actions to take in a hostage situation is to establish a line of communication.

_____ 16. Child stealing is more a crime against a parent or guardian than against a child.

_____ 17. Extortion involves tricking someone into giving money to someone else.

_____ 18. *Blackmail* is another term commonly used to refer to extortion.

_____ 19. The payoff location chosen by an extortionist may be any place that suits the culprit's purpose.

_____ 20. It is not important to obtain fingerprint specimens from suspects in extortion cases.

Key Terms Review

Match the terms with the definitions. Write the letter of the term in the answer column.

a. blackmail
b. kidnapping
c. hostage negotiator
d. Lindbergh law

e. extortion
f. ransom
g. line of communication
h. hostage

_____ 1. Taking another person from one location to another against that person's will, by using force or coercion.

_____ 2. Money, property, or other consideration paid or demanded in exchange for the release of a kidnapped person.

_____ 3. Federal antikidnapping legislation passed in 1932.

_____ 4. An innocent person held captive by one who threatens to kill or harm the person if his or her demands are not met and who uses the person's safety to negotiate for money, property, or escape.

_____ 5. An individual specially trained to deal with persons holding hostages.

_____ 6. A channel for communicating with another party.

7. The obtaining of money or property from another by wrongful use of actual or threatened force, violence, or fear, or under color of official right; refers to such acts by public officials.

8. The unlawful demand of money or property under threat to do bodily harm, to injure property, to accuse of crime, or to expose disgraceful defects; commonly included under extortion statutes.

Applying Concepts

Following are the contents of an unsigned, typed ransom note received at 12:00 noon by SUSAN SOMERS, wife of PHILIP SOMERS, the owner/operator of Colonel Somers Automobile Emporium. The letter was received at home, from an unknown sender. The note was delivered in a sealed white envelope by 13-year-old PETER CONRAD, the local newspaper carrier. CONRAD states that an African-American woman he did not know gave him $20 to deliver the letter. MRS. SOMERS immediately telephoned her husband at work, but she was told he had gone to the country club to play golf at 10:30 A.M. and had not yet returned. At 12:10 P.M., MRS. SOMERS notified the police of what had happened. She also informed headquarters that MR. SOMERS was driving a 1996 aqua-colored Dodge Caravan, with dealer plates I-SELL2U.

After reviewing the contents of the note, make a written list of the actions you would undertake in this investigation.

Text of Typed Ransom Demand

MRS. SOMERS, FOR THE SAFE RETURN OF YOUR HUSBAND, WE ARE DEMANDING $200,000 IN CASH, ALL UNMARKED BILLS. YOU WILL TAKE ALL PRECAUTIONS AGAINST SUSPICION IN DRAWING THE MONEY FROM THE BANK. THE MONEY IS TO BE DELIVERED IN A SPORTS BAG LARGE ENOUGH TO HOLD THIS AMOUNT.

YOU WILL HAVE THE MONEY READY AND BE AT THE INTERSECTION OF MAIN STREET AND EAST PIKE AT EXACTLY 3 P.M. AT EXACTLY 3:10 P.M., WE WILL CALL YOUR CELL PHONE WITH FURTHER INSTRUCTIONS. YOU ARE TO USE YOUR CAR, LICENSE NUMBER MY-BOYS. YOU WILL BE CLOSELY WATCHED ALL THE WAY.

WE KNOW THE PENALTY FOR KIDNAPPING AND WE KNOW WE ARE GAMBLING OUR LIVES. IF YOU WANT TO GAMBLE THE LIFE OF YOUR HUSBAND, CALL IN THE POLICE OR MARK THE MONEY.

DON'T EVEN ENTERTAIN ANY NOTION OF CALLING THE POLICE OR FBI IF YOU EVER WANT TO SEE YOUR HUSBAND AGAIN. SAVE THIS NOTE AND PLACE IT IN THE SPORTS BAG WITH THE MONEY.

_____

_____

_____

_____

_____

CHAPTER 14   Homicide

Study Outline

Homicide and the Law

1. Of all the serious crimes committed, homicide is the one whose _____ demands the greatest effort by the police.

2. Homicide is the killing of one person by _____.

3. Excusable homicides are _____ killings where there is no gross negligence.

4. Most state statutes provide for varying degrees of murder, such as _____-degree and

   second-_____ murder or murder one and murder two.

Motives for Homicide

1. Motive is important in the investigation of a _____.

2. Six possible motives for homicide are:

   a. _____

   b. _____

   c. _____

   d. _____

   e. _____

   f. _____

3. Murder for financial gain often occurs between individuals who have a _____ or contractual relationship or are linked as beneficiaries of a will or an insurance policy.

4. Sexually motivated murders, also sometimes called _____ murders, may be planned and intentional or may occur spontaneously.

5. There are at least _____ forms of what might be called motiveless murders.

The Homicide Investigation

1. Although _____ handle the majority of dead-body calls, patrol officers are often called on to conduct or assist in an investigation involving a death.

2. A person who is near death may appear _____ to an untrained observer.

3. When the investigators arrive at the scene, _____ of them will take charge of all aspects of the case.

4. Knowing who the victim is and how the _____ was killed may provide clues about motive or the suspect's identity.

5. Sometimes a victim may be _____ through his or her personal effects.

6. It is important to _____ the time of death as precisely as possible.

7. Although limp immediately after death, a body stiffens as substances (mainly lactic _____) accumulate in the muscles.

8. Body temperature, though not entirely accurate alone for determining time of _____, can assist in its estimation.

9. The rate of decomposition is influenced by the environment and the _____.

Types of Deaths Investigated and Weapons Used

1. Knowing about the most common kinds of deaths and their characteristics can greatly assist

   _____ investigators.

2. Immediate steps must be taken to _____ the scene and the property of the deceased.

3. Suicide is the intentional _____ of oneself.

4. Suicide is not a criminal offense, but in some jurisdictions, _____ suicide is.

5. The investigation of a suicide is not nearly as _____ or lengthy as the investigation of a homicide.

6. Poisoning is among the _____ methods of murder.

7. A toxicological screening can sometimes reveal the _____ of a toxic substance in a victim.

8. Stabbing and cutting wounds differ in depth, shape, and _____.

9. Gunshot wounds may exhibit certain characteristic entry _____.

10. When a gun is fired while being held against the skin of the victim, a _____ wound results.

11. Death from asphyxiation is an extreme condition caused by a lack of _____ and an excess of carbon dioxide.

12. Most hangings are suicides, but some are _____.

13. Death by drowning results when any _____ enters the breathing passage and prevents the access of air to the lungs.

14. In many states, special statutes apply when death results from the _____ operation of a motor vehicle.

15. As in other deaths, the primary duty of the coroner or medical examiner in a homicide is to determine

the _____ of death.

Concept Review

For each statement, write **T** *in the space provided if the entire statement is true. Write* **F** *if any part of the statement is false.*

___F___ 1. Death investigations that confront the police can be divided into five major categories.

___T___ 2. Homicide is the killing of one person by another.

___T___ 3. Excusable homicides include cases in which one party accidentally kills another without intention or gross negligence.

___T___ 4. Some jurisdictions include the classifications first-degree and second-degree murder, while other jurisdictions do not.

___T___ 5. Motive is an important element in the investigation of a homicide.

___F___ 6. All murders are well-planned activities.

___T___ 7. Some homicides are sexually motivated.

___T___ 8. Some homicides are cases of mistaken identity, although these are not frequent.

___T___ 9. If there is any possibility that a victim may still be alive, an ambulance should be called.

___F___ 10. When people die, their lips sometimes turn green.

___T___ 11. Knowing how a victim was killed may offer clues to a suspect's identity.

___F___ 12. A victim's identity cannot really be determined through examination of the teeth.

___F___ 13. *Rigor mortis* usually does not begin for the first ten hours after death.

___F___ 14. The examination of insects can sometimes assist in determining the cause of death.

___T___ 15. Examining the contents of a deceased person's stomach may assist in determining the time of death.

___F___ 16. Once officers are satisfied that a death was the result of natural causes, there is nothing to do but write a final report.

___F___ 17. Suicides are usually mentally unbalanced people.

___F___ 18. Poisoning is a fairly recent method of committing murder.

_____F__ **19.** Cutting and stabbing wounds appear superficially identical.

_____T__ **20.** Defense wounds usually occur when a victim tries to ward off a stabbing or cutting attack.

Key Terms Review

Match the terms with the definitions. Write the letter of the term in the answer column.

a.	murder	**k.**	forensic pathology
b.	cadaveric spasm	**l.**	toxicological screening
c.	wipe ring	**m.**	justifiable homicide
d.	homicide	**n.**	forensic entomologist
e.	autoerotic asphyxiation	**o.**	criminal homicide
f.	defense wound	**p.**	*livor mortis*
g.	adipocere	**q.**	felony murder
h.	manslaughter	**r.**	*rigor mortis*
i.	asphyxiation	**s.**	tattooing
j.	excusable homicide	**t.**	contact wound

___D___ **1.** The killing of one human being by another.

___M___ **2.** The killing of another in self-defense or defense of others when danger of death or serious bodily injury exists.

___J___ **3.** The killing of a human being without intention and where there is no gross negligence.

___O___ **4.** The wrongful killing of a human being without justification or excuse in the law. There are two degrees of the offense—murder and manslaughter.

___A___ **5.** The unlawful killing of a human being by another with malice aforethought.

___Q___ **6.** The killing of a person during the commission or attempted commission of a felony other than murder.

___H___ **7.** The unlawful killing of another without malice. It may be voluntary—upon sudden heat of passion—or involuntary—in the commission of an unlawful act.

___K___ **8.** A specialized field of medicine that studies and interprets, in relation to crime investigation, changes in body tissues and fluids.

___R___ **9.** A stiffening of the body after death that disappears over time.

___B___ **10.** A rigidity of certain muscles usually occurring when the victim is holding something at the time of death and the hand closes tightly around the object; sometimes a sign of suicide.

___P___ **11.** A dark discoloration of the body where blood has pooled or drained to the lowest level; also called *postmortem lividity*.

___G___ **12.** A whitish gray, soapy or waxy substance that forms on the surface of a body left for weeks in a damp location.

___N___ **13.** A person who specializes in the study of insects in relation to determining the location, time, and cause of death.

___L___ **14.** An examination of body tissue or fluids for poisons or other toxins.

_C_ **15.** A gray ring around a gunshot wound, resulting from the deposit of gunpowder by a gun blast at close range.

_S_ **16.** The burned skin around a gunshot wound, resulting from hot gunpowder from a gun blast at very close range.

_F_ **17.** A wound on the hand or forearm of a victim who has attempted to fend off an attack.

_I_ **18.** A wound created when a gun is fired while being held against the skin of the victim; typically found in self-inflicted wounds and execution-type murders.

_I_ **19.** Death due to a lack of oxygen and an excess of carbon dioxide in the blood.

_E_ **20.** The seeking of sexual gratification by near asphyxia.

Applying Concepts

Prepare a description and list of the things you would do to conduct an investigation of the case described below. Assume that you have just arrived at the scene. In your description, include identification of leads that you want covered and the information you hope to obtain as a result of such coverage. Your investigation should be logical, thorough, and systematic. All activities should be conducted in accordance with proven investigative practices.

The Case

At 1300 hours, a call is received from Deborah Sugar, proprietor of the Do Drop Inn, a 20-unit group of rental cottages. The inn is located on the edge of Center City at the intersection of Water Street and Highway 80. Sugar says that she believes that someone in cottage 9 has been shot. She identifies the renter of cottage 9 as Arnold Schwartz, a 32-year-old bartender who works a night shift at the Colonial Tavern on Highway 80. Sugar states, "Arny likes to play the horses." Sugar states that she heard what she believes to be the sound of three shots coming from cottage 9. Shortly thereafter she saw an unknown man run to a 1996 gold four-door Toyota Camry sedan and drive it out of the parking lot hurriedly. He headed north on Highway 80 toward Solomon Homes. Sugar is able to furnish a partial license plate number: 13 _ _ _ G. Sugar describes the suspect as a white male, 30–35 years old, with thick brown bushy hair, a tanned complexion, and a full face, wearing a dark brown suit coat and a pastel yellow sport shirt. Sugar believes she might be able to recognize the suspect.

After this information is received, the following broadcast is made: "Unit 15A, see the woman at Do Drop Inn, on Water Street and Highway 80. Shot fired." Unit 15A acknowledges the broadcast.

The weather is clear and sunny. On arrival at the scene, you and your partner (an investigative team assigned to Homicide), observe six cars parked in the lot of the Do Drop Inn. Ms. Sugar meets you and your partner in the driveway and points out cottage 9. Approaching this cottage, you note that the door has been opened about 4 inches. You push it open all the way with your knee. Just inside the door, you observe the body of a man lying on the hardwood floor face up, head to the north. His eyes and mouth are partially open. The victim has on gray slacks, a white shirt, black shoes, and black socks. Sugar readily identifies the person as Mr. Schwartz, the renter of the unit.

You observe bloodstains on the victim's shirt and near the heart, and a small pool of blood on the floor near the victim's left armpit. You also note an overturned lamp, chair, and coffee table. The glass top of the coffee table is broken into several pieces. These are all evidence of an apparent struggle. Around the body, you observe several items: a chrome cigarette lighter, a black pocket comb, a square shirt button, a half-used book of matches with a lion insignia on the cover, an open black wallet apparently empty except for several identification cards, and several cigarette butts (Camel brand). On the north side of the lamp table, next to the sofa, you note a half-full bottle of what appears to be Johnny Walker red-label Scotch whisky, with two glasses. A walnut-finish rolltop desk in the northwest corner of the room appears to have been ransacked. Many pieces of paper are strewn around it on the floor.

The only bedroom is in the northwest corner of the cottage. The dressers have been left partly open. Other areas of the cottage seem normal. Just outside the front door, to the left as you enter, you notice a .38 caliber revolver, partly hidden by a large shrub. You also observe one identifiable footprint.

CHAPTER 15   Burglary

Study Outline

The Nature of Burglary

1. Burglaries are among the most _____ crimes to solve.

2. Since victims seldom see the burglar and a time lag may interfere, investigators must establish the *corpus delicti* (essential elements) of the crime through largely _____ evidence.

Legal Aspects of the Crime of Burglary

1. In common _____, the offense of burglary was defined as the breaking and entering of a dwelling house of another in the nighttime, with _____ to commit a felony therein.

2. Entry into the dwelling has been interpreted as the insertion of any or all of the accused's _____ into the dwelling.

3. A crime may be classified as _____ and entering rather than burglary to further distinguish the criminal act.

Types of Burglaries

1. There are two primary ways to classify burglaries:

   a. _____

   b. _____

2. Commercial burglaries are those that occur in nonresidential buildings or structures where some form of commerce _____ place.

3. In many cases, _____ burglaries are better planned than residential ones.

The Burglar—Trade and Tools

1. The _____ in which burglars operate are quite varied.

2. Opportunistic burglars drive around residential communities looking for _____ targets.

3. The tools chosen by burglars usually _____ on the method of entry and the type of burglary planned.

Criminal Investigation—Study Guide **81**

Investigating Burglaries

1. A thorough knowledge of the _____ used by burglars is essential to an effective investigation.

2. Remember that some types of evidence may have latent or microscopic _____.

3. If K-9 units are available in the area, it is advisable to request their assistance in searching large stores or warehouses during alarm _____.

4. Ideally, a burglary investigation should involve more than a _____ officer.

5. When searching the scene of a burglary, officers should seek the manner and method of both _____ and exit.

6. Investigators should be alert for any unusual events or disturbances _____ at the scene.

7. Whenever burglary suspects are apprehended, they should be immediately advised of their _____ under *Miranda.*

Safe Burglaries

1. Generally, safes can be divided into two classifications:

   a. _____

   b. _____

2. Burglars use a number of methods to _____ entry into safes.

3. Chopping is a rather _____ way to attack a safe.

4. Safe burglars usually work in groups of _____ or more.

5. Because safe burglars take such _____ precautions, it is unlikely that any evidence found at the scene will immediately _____ the burglar.

Concept Review

For each statement, write **T** *in the space provided if the entire statement is true. Write* **F** *if any part of the statement is false.*

_____ 1. Nearly 40 percent of all burglaries in 1995 were residential.

_____ 2. Burglaries are among the most difficult crimes to solve.

_____ 3. Force and fear are necessary in the *corpus delicti* of burglary.

_____ 4. A robbery in a trailer would be an example of a commercial burglary.

_____ 5. A man entering a convenience store with a gun and ordering the proprietor to give him the money in the cash register is an example of a commercial burglary.

_____ 6. Package burglars feign a parcel or package delivery to determine if anyone is home.

_____ 7. It is not uncommon for someone with financial problems to stage a fake burglary for the insurance money.

_____ 8. Some burglary tools are specialized tools used by locksmiths and have little other use.

_____ 9. When answering a burglary call, an officer should not worry about people standing around outside the crime scene.

_____ 10. A diagonal deployment requires at least two officers.

_____ 11. If K-9 units are available in an area, they should be summoned to undertake searches of large buildings during a burglary call.

_____ 12. Unlike most other criminal investigations, burglary investigations do not require one to secure the crime scene.

_____ 13. Burglary suspects, when apprehended, are not afforded the same constitutional rights as other types of suspects.

_____ 14. All burglarproof safes are also fire-resistant.

_____ 15. Safe burglars usually work alone.

Key Terms Review

Match the terms with the definitions. Write the letter of the term in the answer column.

a. jimmy
b. burglary
c. nonalarm call
d. commercial burglary

e. diagonal deployment
f. residential burglary
g. burglary tools
h. alarm call

_____ 1. Entering a building or occupied structure, without the consent of the person in possession, to commit a crime therein.

_____ 2. A burglary committed at a dwelling place, whether occupied or vacant.

_____ 3. A burglary committed at a place of business or commerce.

_____ 4. A prying tool of any sort, used to force open a door, window, or lock.

_____ 5. Any of an assortment of tools and picks that may be used in committing a burglary.

_____ 6. Notification of the police by audible or silent alarm that a crime such as a break-in has occurred.

_____ 7. Notification of the police by citizen alert or direct observation that a crime such as a break-in has occurred.

_____ 8. A method of arranging officers to both secure and observe a crime scene. Officers arrange themselves so that each can observe two sides of a building at once.

Applying Concepts

1. Describe each of the following methods of safe breaking, and explain why a safe burglar might employ the method.

   a. Ripping and peeling: _____

   _____

   _____

   _____

   _____

   _____

   _____

   _____

   _____

   _____

   b. Chopping: _____

   _____

   _____

   _____

   _____

   _____

   _____

   _____

   _____

   _____

   _____

c. Explosives:_____

_____

_____

_____

_____

_____

_____

_____

_____

_____

2. What is the *modus operandi* in each of the following types of burglary?

a. Burglary during a party:_____

_____

_____

_____

_____

_____

_____

_____

_____

_____

_____

_____

_____

_____

b. Invading burglary: _____

_____

_____

_____

_____

_____

_____

_____

_____

_____

_____

_____

c. Window smashing: _____

_____

_____

_____

_____

_____

_____

_____

_____

_____

_____

_____

_____

CHAPTER 16   Larceny/Theft

Study Outline

The Nature of Larceny/Theft

1. Larceny/theft is the most common _____ of gain.

2. Thieves may be _____ or old, male or _____, rich or poor, employed or

   _____, and from any race, religion, or social status.

Legal Aspects of Larceny/Theft

1. Theft, the taking of property without the owner's consent, is a _____ name for larceny and is frequently used as a synonym.

2. In general, modern statutes retain the ancient English classification of degrees of _____, based on the value of the items taken.

Types of Larceny/Theft

1. Pickpockets may work _____ or in small groups.

2. Pickpockets sometimes use a bumping _____.

3. Traditional pickpockets are considered to be among the most _____ mechanical criminals.

4. Shoplifting accounts for nearly _____ percent of all retail losses in the United States each year.

5. Shoplifting, the taking of goods from a _____ establishment without paying for them, generally occurs while the person is posing as a customer.

Fraud

1. Fraud is misrepresentation, trickery, or deception with criminal intent to _____ someone of his or her property.

2. The use of stolen, forged, or unauthorized credit cards or credit card _____ has become a huge illegal business.

3. Check _____ is the attempt to pass off a false signature on a check as genuine.

4. The confidence artist's business is to stimulate the interest and _____ of the victim until his or her reason, judgment, and logic are overwhelmed.

5. Some carnival games of chance are run _____.

6. Fraud contributes significantly to America's insurance _____ each year.

7. Ponzi schemes are named for _____ Ponzi, who bilked thousands of Bostonians of their money.

8. Telemarketing fraud and other types of fraud using the telephone have _____ in recent years.

9. Of course, not all solicitations made through the mail or over the telephone are _____.

Receiving Stolen Property

1. Although statutes vary across the nation, they rarely, if ever, classify mere _____ of stolen property as a crime.

2. *Fence* is the popular name for a go-between who knowingly receives and disposes of _____ property.

3. A fencing operation may be small and simple or _____ and complex.

4. Periodically, police agencies establish fencing _____ operations.

5. It has been long established that one way to inhibit fencing is to place _____ numbers on products.

Concept Review

*For each statement, write **T** in the space provided if the entire statement is true. Write **F** if any part of the statement is false.*

_____ 1. Thieves come in all ages, races, and types of people.

_____ 2. Theft is the taking of property with or without the owner's consent.

_____ 3. Most statutes today classify thefts as petty larceny and grand larceny.

_____ 4. Pickpockets may work alone or in small groups.

_____ 5. Some pickpockets operate simply by cutting people's pockets and letting the contents fall out.

_____ 6. Shoplifters account for 50 percent of all retail losses in the United States each year.

_____ 7. Most amateur shoplifters simply try to conceal merchandise in a shopping bag, purse, pocket, backpack, or coat or under clothing.

_____ 8. A common target of shoplifters is meat from grocery stores.

_____ 9. Professional shoplifters tend to be more imaginative than amateurs, and their motive is profit.

_____ 10. Shoplifting is a form of fraud.

_____ 11. The "mark" is another name for the victim of a con game.

_____ 12. The pigeon-drop bunco is operated by at least two con artists.

_____ 13. Three-card Monte is the name of a notorious bunco artist.

_____ 14. All carnival games are dishonest.

_____ 15. Many of the notifications people receive in the mail indicating awards of prizes are actually swindles.

Key Terms Review

Match the terms with the definitions. Write the letter of the term in the answer column.

a. shill
b. booster device
c. petty larceny
d. theft
e. sting operation
f. grand larceny

g. employee pilfering
h. hang paper
i. larceny/theft
j. fraud
k. shoplifting
l. fence

_____ 1. The taking of property without the owner's consent; a popular term for larceny.

_____ 2. The taking and carrying, leading, riding, or driving away of the personal property of another with the specific intent of permanently depriving the owner of his or her property.

_____ 3. The taking and carrying away of another's personal property with a value in excess of a cut-off amount in a given jurisdiction, with the intent of depriving the owner of it permanently; generally considered a felony.

_____ 4. The taking and carrying away of another's personal property with a value below the cutoff amount in a given jurisdiction, with the intent of depriving the owner of it permanently; generally considered a misdemeanor.

_____ 5. The taking of goods from a retail establishment without paying for them, while posing as a customer.

_____ 6. The theft of goods from warehouses, factories, and offices by employees.

_____ 7. A container, generally a box, with a spring-loaded trapdoor, allowing the professional shoplifter to conceal stolen goods.

_____ 8. Slang term for a professional receiver, concealer, and disburser of stolen property.

_____ 9. Misrepresentation, trickery, or deception with criminal intent to deprive someone of his or her property.

_____ 10. To intentionally write bad checks; slang expression.

_____ 11. A slang term for a secret coconspirator or accomplice in a confidence game.

_____ 12. An undercover operation set up by law enforcement personnel to catch, or "sting," offenders committing a crime; often used to collect evidence against thieves.

Criminal Investigation—Study Guide

Applying Concepts

1. Create a list of the confidence games or bunco crimes that might occur in your local community. Explain why these particular types of crimes might occur.

_____

_____

_____

_____

_____

_____

_____

_____

_____

_____

_____

2. What are some of the things merchants can do to avoid receiving bad or fraudulent checks?

_____

_____

_____

_____

_____

_____

_____

_____

_____

_____

_____

CHAPTER 17   Motor Vehicle Theft

Study Outline

The Nature of Motor Vehicle Theft

1. Automobile theft has traditionally been a major problem in _____ American cities.

2. Cars have been stolen from every conceivable place: homes, shopping malls, main streets, _____ streets, parking lots and garages, and even right off the sales floors of dealerships.

Types of Motor Vehicle Theft

1. Motor vehicle thefts are generally classified by the _____ motive for stealing the vehicle.

2. For the most part, these motives may be divided into five major categories:

   a. _____

   b. _____

   c. _____

   d. _____

   e. _____

3. Teenagers who steal a car simply to drive around and then abandon it account for most _____.

4. Some offenders steal a car to use as _____ when committing another crime.

5. Some vehicles are _____ for the purpose of stripping them of valuable parts and accessories for resale or for sale to wrecking yards.

6. A _____ shop is a place where stolen vehicles are taken for chopping or dismantling into parts or accessories that cannot be easily identified.

Legal Aspects of the Crime of Motor Vehicle Theft

1. Prosecution for _____ vehicle theft varies among the states.

2. To combat motor vehicle theft, states have enacted a variety of _____ that require stiffer penalties for motor-vehicle-related crimes.

Investigating Motor Vehicle Theft

1. Once the police have received notification of a vehicle theft, they respond to the _____, obtain all pertinent information, and write a formal report.

2. The investigating officer must also verify that a _____ has taken place.

3. Having accurate information in the theft report does not ensure that the _____ will be recovered.

4. Even when a vehicle that matches the make, model, year, and color of a stolen vehicle has been recovered, it may not be the _____ vehicle.

5. To assure that the right vehicle has been found, the investigator relies on _____ numbers affixed to or inscribed on various parts of the car.

6. When verifying the VIN of an automobile suspected of being stolen, look for signs indicating that the _____ plate has been damaged or disturbed.

7. With experience on the street, an investigator develops an instinct or _____ sense about stolen cars.

8. Thieves gain _____ to and start vehicles by a number of different methods.

9. The immediate area where a car is recovered becomes the _____ scene.

10. If a stolen vehicle is to be processed for fingerprints, searched for possible evidence, or examined by a forensic technician, it is _____.

Investigating Other Motor Vehicle Thefts

1. During the past 10 or 15 years, the theft of motorcycles has been _____ along with their popularity.

2. Motorcycles are typically stolen for _____ or resale.

Preventing Motor Vehicle Theft

1. Generally, the theft of a vehicle requires _____ things—a desire on the part of the thief and an opportunity, sometimes inadvertently provided by the owner.

2. Each year, numerous law enforcement agencies try to reduce the number of vehicle thefts in their _____.

3. Some jurisdictions have set up _____ alert programs.

Concept Review

For each statement, write **T** *in the space provided if the entire statement is true. Write* **F** *if any part of the statement is false.*

_____ 1. Only large cities have serious problems with vehicle thefts.

_____ 2. Most cars are stolen from shopping malls.

_____ 3. Joyriding is typically undertaken by juveniles.

_____ 4. Hitchhikers usually steal cars in order to go joyriding.

_____ 5. It is common for a bank robber to steal a car to use in his or her getaway.

_____ 6. In regard to car theft, *stripping* refers to lifting the top coat of paint from a vehicle.

_____ 7. Sometimes automobile strippers seek out specific models and particular parts.

_____ 8. Chopping of cars is usually undertaken in a chop shop.

_____ 9. Provided the police have accurate information for their reports, they are assured of recovering the stolen vehicle.

_____ 10. It is not always the most expensive or best-looking car that gets stolen.

_____ 11. Today, VIN plates are usually found on the right-hand side of the dashboard.

_____ 12. Observing a commercial license plate on a passenger car might alert an officer to a stolen car.

_____ 13. One valuable source of vehicle theft information is the FBI's NCIC.

_____ 14. Motorcycles are typically stolen for personal use by the thief.

_____ 15. An impounded vehicle is one held by the police for technical or forensic examination.

Key Terms Review

Match the terms with the definitions. Write the letter of the term in the answer column.

a. vehicle identification
    number (VIN)
b. salvage switch
c. impound
d. motor vehicle theft

e. chop shop
f. slim Jim
g. joyriding
h. chopping
i. stripping

_____ **1.** The theft or attempted theft of a motor vehicle.

_____ **2.** The temporary taking of a motor vehicle without the intent of permanently depriving the owner of the vehicle; generally undertaken by juveniles.

_____ **3.** A switching of vehicle identification number plates from wrecked vehicles to stolen cars of the same make and model.

_____ **4.** Illegally removing parts and accessories from motor vehicles to use or sell them.

_____ **5.** A place for chopping, or dismantling, stolen motor vehicles into parts and accessories that cannot be easily identified, which are resold.

_____ **6.** The dismantling of stolen motor vehicles into parts and accessories for use or sale.

_____ **7.** A nonduplicated, serialized number assigned by a motor vehicle manufacturer (of autos, especially) to each vehicle made.

_____ **8.** A tool, consisting of a sturdy length of metal, used by auto and truck thieves to unlock doors.

_____ **9.** To take into legal custody.

Applying Concepts

List some of the precautions that average citizens can take to prevent their cars from being stolen.

_____

_____

_____

_____

_____

_____

_____

_____

_____

_____

CHAPTER 18   Arson and Bombing Investigations

Study Outline

The Crime of Arson

1. Estimates of total property loss each year for all arsons range from $1.5 billion to $_____ billion.

2. Detection and _____ of arson cases are extremely difficult.

Legal Elements of the Crime of Arson

1. Arson is a combination crime against _____ and property.

2. In most jurisdictions, _____ broadly covers the burning of all kinds of buildings and structures, as well as crops, forests, farm equipment, and personal property such as boats, cars, and other vehicles.

3. Some jurisdictions categorize an arson as aggravated or _____.

4. In addition to aggravated and simple arson, most jurisdictions define a lesser crime known as

   _____ arson.

Motives for Arson

1. Motive is _____ an element of the crime of arson—nor of any other crime, for that matter.

2. Motives can provide compelling explanations for the court or the jury, helping them understand

   _____ the accused committed the crime.

Investigating Arson

1. Once a fire is out, the investigator must determine where and how the fire_____.

2. Investigating arson differs from investigating _____ previously discussed in the textbook.

3. Since arson does not have an immediately apparent _____ delicti, it is the responsibility of the investigator to show that a particular fire occurred and that it was deliberately set.

4. The fire triangle is composed of three basic elements—air or oxygen, _____, and heat.

5. Burn _____ show the effects of burning or partial burning during the fire.

6. Often these patterns provide clues to where the _____ was ignited.

7. Irregular cracks and lines produced in glass and ceramic materials by rapid, intense heat are known as _____.

8. Evidence of an accelerant found at the point of _____ of a fire is a primary form of physical evidence.

9. Different agencies, often with joint _____, investigate suspicious fires.

10. As a general rule of thumb, it is the _____ department's role to determine the nature and origin of the burning.

Criminal Bombing

1. Bombing incidents, like _____ incidents, destroy property and take innocent lives.

2. Bombing incidents are generally divided into explosive bombings and _____ bombings.

3. The main function of any law enforcement agency in a bombing incident is to protect human _____ and property, remove the bomb menace if possible, and investigate and apprehend the _____ or threateners.

4. An explosive is any _____ that produces a rapid, violent reaction when subjected to heat or a strong blow or shock.

5. Among the materials classified as high _____, the rate of change to a gas is very rapid.

6. When searching the site of a bombing, an investigator must try to find _____ of the mechanism used to detonate the bomb.

7. Safety fuses convey a _____ through a medium at a continuous and uniform rate to a nonelectric blasting cap.

Types of Bombs

1. The police must deal with many types of _____ and incendiary devices.

2. Contrary to popular opinion, neither commercial explosives nor blasting caps are needed to construct highly effective _____.

3. Black _____ or smokeless powder is frequently used to load pipebombs, one of the most common types of bombs police encounter.

4. Some bombs are created to induce burning. The crudest of these is the _____ cocktail.

5. Letter and _____ bombs are rare but particularly disturbing.

6. Package bombs also vary widely in size, weight, shape, and the _____ of the wrapping.

7. Some criminals use bombs as _____ traps.

Investigating Bombing Incidents

1. Actions taken in bombing incidents are controlled by the characteristics of the actual or

   _____ bomb.

2. Bomb searches are typically conducted by _____-person teams.

3. The primary objects of an investigation following the explosion of a bomb are as follows:

   a. _____

   b. _____

   c. _____

Concept Review

For each statement, write **T** *in the space provided if the entire statement is true. Write* **F** *if any part of the statement is false.*

___T___ **1.** Arson is an index crime.

___F___ **2.** Arson is chiefly a crime against property.

___F___ **3.** The fire department always has exclusive jurisdiction over arson investigations.

___T___ **4.** Arson is frequently divided into two categories, namely, aggravated and simple.

___T___ **5.** Simple arson is the intentional burning of property without creating an imminent risk to human life.

___T___ **6.** Convictions can be obtained in arson cases even when no motive can be shown.

___T___ **7.** The determination that the crime of arson has occurred happens either while the fire is burning or after it has been extinguished.

___F___ **8.** Typically, investigators begin their investigation of a suspicious fire by examining the inside of a structure.

___F___ **9.** The fire triangle is composed of air or oxygen, water, and heat.

___F___ **10.** The typical fire pattern one finds on the wall of a home fireplace is spalling.

___T___ **11.** Pour or spill patterns are usually caused by the pouring of an accelerant.

___F___ **12.** Black smoke at the beginning of a fire usually means that paper was used to start the fire.

___T___ **13.** In some larger cities, arson is investigated by special units from the fire and police departments.

___F___ **14.** Bombing incidents are generally divided into explosive bombings and explosive killings.

___F___ **15.** An explosive is any material that produces a shattering expansion of gas.

___T___ **16.** High explosives require some shock to detonate them.

___T___ **17.** Low explosives deflagrate, rather than explode.

___T___ **18.** Pipebombs are among the most common bombs encountered by police.

___F___ **19.** Letter bombs can usually be easily detected by the postal service.

___F___ **20.** Bomb searches are usually undertaken by teams of three or more officers.

Key Terms Review

Match the terms with the definitions. Write the letter of the term in the answer column.

a.	explosive	**j.**	high explosive
b.	delayed ignition	**k.**	accelerant
c.	attempted arson	**l.**	trailer
d.	aggravated arson	**m.**	simple arson
e.	low explosive	**n.**	bombing
f.	spalling	**o.**	crazing
g.	incendiary fire	**p.**	fire triangle
h.	arson	**q.**	direct ignition
i.	alligatoring		

___H___ **1.** The malicious and intentional or fraudulent burning of buildings or property.

___D___ **2.** The malicious, intentional burning of buildings or property and knowingly creating an imminent danger to human life or a risk of great bodily harm to others.

___M___ **3.** The malicious, intentional burning of buildings or property that does not create an imminent risk or threat to human life.

___C___ **4.** The demonstrated intent to set a fire coupled with some overt act toward actually setting the fire.

___K___ **5.** A booster such as gasoline, kerosene, or paint thinner added to a fire to speed its progress.

___G___ **6.** A fire in which a fire-setting device, an igniter, or an accelerant is found.

___P___ **7.** The three basic elements—oxygen, fuel, and heat—needed for a fire.

___Q___ **8.** Setting a fire by directly applying a flame.

___B___ **9.** Setting a fire indirectly by means of a mechanical, chemical, or other timing device.

___I___ **10.** A scalelike burn pattern on wood. Large scales indicate rapid, intense heat; small, flat scales indicate low-intensity heat over a long period of time.

___O___ **11.** Irregular cracks and lines in glass and ceramic materials, caused by rapid, intense heat.

_F_ **12.** The chipping, crumbling, or flaking of cement or masonry caused by rapid, intense heat.

_L_ **13.** A material (rope or rags soaked in accelerant, shredded paper, gunpowder, fluid accelerant, and so on) used to spread a fire.

_N_ **14.** An incident in which a device constructed with criminal intent and using high explosives, low explosives, or blasting agents explodes.

_A_ **15.** Any material that produces a rapid, violent reaction when subjected to heat or a strong blow or shock.

_J_ **16.** An explosive material in which the rate of change to a gas is very rapid; explodes only by the shock of a blasting cap, a detonating cord, or an electric detonator; includes nitroglycerin, TNT, RDX, and plastic explosives.

_E_ **17.** An explosive material in which the rate of change to a gas is quite slow; the material deflagrates, or burns rapidly, rather than explodes; includes black powder, smokeless powder, and fertilizers.

Applying Concepts

Consider the information set forth in the following two problems, and describe the procedures you would follow, given each problem's conditions and situations. Obviously, you would notify headquarters. However, what else would you do to save lives and protect property? For example, in problem 1, exactly how would you get the people out of the theater without causing panic? What else must be done?

1. At 1900 hours, you are patrolling Main Street in downtown Cedarville. A tall man wearing an orange sports jacket flags down your unit in front of King's Multiplex Theater at 605 North Main Street. The man is very excited. He identifies himself as the manager of King's Multiplex Theater, and he tells you that he thinks there may be a small fire in the basement. He says he doesn't know what to do, since all four of the theaters are full of people. He is afraid to call the fire department and frighten the theatergoers into a panic. He thinks that the fire is contained in the corner of a storage room in the basement and that there may be little more than some stacked papers stored down there.

_____

_____

_____

_____

_____

_____

_____

_____

_____

_____

_____

_____

_____

_____

_____

2. At 1330 hours, an unknown man enters the Food Fair Supermarket, carrying a package wrapped in plain brown paper with a white envelope attached to the top with cellophane tape. The envelope is addressed to Douglas J. Miller, manager of the market. Miller opens the envelope and notes that the letter was apparently typed on a manual typewriter (the print is slightly uneven and inconsistent in tone). The note reads as follows:

I hate this store! You are a filthy thief who sells overpriced low-quality products. There is a bomb in this package, and it will go off in 20 minutes. There are ten sticks of dynamite in this package, and that should blow your whole store to hell. I only hope you try to open the package and stop the bomb. Then you can be blown to hell too!!!!!!!

Mr. Miller calls the station, and you are immediately dispatched. You arrive 5 minutes later. The clock is ticking.

_____

_____

_____

_____

_____

_____

_____

_____

_____

_____

_____

_____

_____

CHAPTER 19   Organized Crime

Study Outline

What Is Organized Crime?

1. The term *organized crime* conjures up images of large men in _____ suits, secret rituals, meetings of family members, and gangland killings.

2. The definition and understanding of what constitutes organized crime _____.

3. Organized crime groups are shrouded in _____, wield enormous power, and have fabulous wealth.

4. Organized crime groups like the Mafia have a formal _____ structure similar to that of many corporations.

Organized Crime Groups

1. Many organized crime groups are offshoots of _____ gangs that formed out of a need for association, protection, and defense against political, economic, and social isolation.

2. La Cosa Nostra is the best-known organized crime group operating in the _____ States today.

3. When the Great Depression hit in 1929, the Mafia was rolling in money from illegal _____.

4. Posses, named after the vigilante groups in the cheap European Westerns popular in _____, originated in Kingston, the capital city.

5. Asian _____ groups run the gamut from Chinese triads to Viet Ching.

6. Tongs began as benevolent societies set up along family or business lines in major American _____ with large Chinese populations.

7. The Yakuza had their origins in the customs and traditions of the _____ warrior class of ancient Japan.

8. At the close of the Vietnam War in the late 1970s, many Vietnamese began migrating to other _____.

9. The breakup of the Soviet _____ in 1991 brought Russian and Eastern European gangsters out of the underground.

10. During the late 1950s and early _____, youthful street gangs were problems only in several large American cities.

11. Today, _____ gangs are involved in murder, drug trafficking, and a host of other serious crimes.

Investigating Organized Crime

1. Since the early _____, law enforcement agencies investigating organized crime have relied on the enterprise theory of investigation.

2. The crimes outlined in RICO are referred to as predicate crimes because they constitute a

_____, or basis, for a violation of the statute.

3. One very effective technique for investigating organized crime has been the creation of organized

crime _____ forces.

4. Many _____ regard electronic surveillance as one of the most effective methods of gathering evidence against notorious mobsters.

5. The Hobbs Act is an _____ act legislated during the 1940s.

6. The Comprehensive Crime Control Act of 1984 was yet another attempt to squelch drug and

_____ crime activities in the United States.

The Future of Organized Crime

1. Patterns in organized crime suggest that the traditional _____ organized crime family is on the decline.

2. The future of investigation of criminal organizations is likely to remain in the area of money

_____ and misuse of electronic transfers of funds between financial institutions.

Concept Review

*For each statement, write **T** in the space provided if the entire statement is true. Write **F** if any part of the statement is false.*

_____ 1. The general public associates the idea of organized crime with the Mafia.

_____ 2. Organized crime groups like the Mafia have no formal organizational structure.

_____ 3. Many organized crime groups originated as ethnic gangs bent on protection and defense against political, economic, and social isolation.

_____ 4. La Cosa Nostra originated in Northern Italy.

_____ 5. The Mafia originally made most of its wealth in gambling and drugs.

_____ 6. The Colombian cartels have been almost completely eradicated.

_____ 7. Jamaican posses originated in Kingston, the capital city.

_____ 8. Jamaican posses are among the most sophisticated crack dealers in the United States.

_____ 9. In addition to being profit-oriented, Jamaican posses are also politically motivated.

_____ 10. Triads are actually the oldest of the organized crime groups, having come into being in the late 1600s.

_____ 11. Tongs began as violent, rebellious ethnic gangs.

_____ 12. The Yakuza can be recognized by a particular hairstyle they always wear.

_____ 13. The Yakuza trace their origins back to the traditions of the samurai warriors of ancient Japan.

_____ 14. The Viet Ching formed small gangs that preyed largely on Asian communities.

_____ 15. Russian and Eastern European gangs did not operate in North America until after the fall of the Soviet Union in 1991.

_____ 16. The Chips and the Bloods are two nationally organized youth gangs.

_____ 17. Most early motorcycle gangs had members who were war veterans.

_____ 18. The RICO statute requires a pattern of racketeering activity.

_____ 19. Electronic surveillance is an important tool for investigating organized criminal groups.

_____ 20. The future of investigation of organized crime lies mainly in the area of money laundering.

Key Terms Review

Match the terms with the definitions. Write the letter of the term in the answer column.

a. injunction
b. recalcitrant witness
c. money laundering
d. undercover operation
e. organized crime
f. conspiracy

g. absolute immunity
h. enterprise theory of investigation
i. predicate crime
j. informer
k. forfeiture

_____ **1.** A highly structured, disciplined, self-perpetuating association of people, usually bound by ethnic ties, who conspire to commit crimes for profit and use fear and corruption to protect their activities from criminal prosecution.

_____ **2.** The investing of illegally obtained money into businesses and real estate that are operated and maintained within the law.

_____ **3.** An approach to criminal investigation that targets entire crime organizations instead of individual criminals within them.

_____ **4.** A crime that is a basis of a violation of the RICO statute.

_____ **5.** The loss of money and/or property to the state as a criminal sanction.

_____ **6.** A court order prohibiting a party from a specific course of action or ordering a party to perform some action.

_____ **7.** A member of an organized crime group who provides information and testimony for law enforcement investigations and prosecutions.

_____ **8.** An investigative police operation designed to secretly uncover evidence against organized crime groups.

_____ **9.** A guarantee that, as long as a witness complies with the court and testifies, the testimony cannot be used against him or her in any criminal action.

_____ **10.** A witness who refuses to testify in a criminal proceeding, even after being offered immunity.

_____ **11.** A crime in which two or more parties are in concert in a criminal purpose.

Applying Concepts

Explain how each of the following descriptions might suggest organized criminal activity.

1. A motel on the highway appears to have a fairly brisk business, but patrons do not seem to have much luggage when they check in. Moreover, few patrons seem to stay overnight.

_____

_____

_____

_____

_____

_____

_____

2. A local hobby shop has sparsely filled shelves, and its items are all very overpriced. Yet, there is frequent activity in the shop, and many people come and go—without any sales being rung up on the register.

_____

_____

_____

_____

_____

_____

_____

3. A restaurant believed to be owned by local criminals is burned to the ground one night. No one is injured. The fire is ruled suspicious.

_____

_____

_____

_____

_____

_____

4. A group of people frequent a local bar, although none of them live in the area.

_____

_____

_____

_____

_____

_____

5. A man makes regular rounds to several local businesses. He enters each business empty-handed and buys nothing, yet he exits each with a small paper bag.

_____

_____

_____

_____

_____

_____

6. A group of young men appears on or near the same street corner each day, and they hang out, talking, for hours. None appear to have jobs, yet they all dress well and leave the area driving late-model cars.

_____

_____

_____

_____

_____

_____

CHAPTER 20   White-Collar Crime

Study Outline

What Is White-Collar Crime?

1. Typically, when referring to white-collar crimes, one is talking about _____-related or occupational crimes.

2. In fact, even certain variations of traditional frauds and _____ discussed in Chapter 16 fit the definition of a white-collar crime.

3. The enforcement of laws concerning white-collar offenses differs from traditional law _____.

4. Historically, _____ enforcement has virtually ignored many aspects of white-collar crime.

Identifying White-Collar Crimes

1. The first category, occupational crime, includes all offenses _____ by individuals

    in the course of their occupation and by _____ against their employers.

2. The second category, _____ crime, involves "the offenses committed by corporate

    officials for the corporation and the offenses of the _____ itself."

3. Another way to look at white-collar crimes is as Herbert Edelhertz did, by dividing these behaviors into four distinct categories:

    a. _____

    b. _____

    c. _____

    d. _____

4. Abuses of trust include any _____ of authority or malfeasance or public corruption

    committed by an individual in a place of _____ in an organization or government.

5. Disguise of purpose refers to the offender's _____ while carrying out the scheme.

Types of White-Collar Crime

1. Embezzlement is usually thought of as a theft committed by an individual against his or her _____.

2. Not all embezzlement or organizational theft, however, occurs at the _____.

3. Recently, insider _____ in stocks and bonds has become a serious criminal problem.

4. Though similar, bribes, kickbacks, and payoffs are not _____.

5. Perhaps the most common form of white-collar criminality is tax cheating or _____ evasion.

6. Since the beginning of the nineteenth _____, certain business practices have been defined in the law as illegal.

Investigating White-Collar Crime

1. When white-collar crimes are detected, they may not always be reported to the _____.

2. On the federal level, _____ of white-collar crime is left chiefly to administrative _____ and regulatory agencies.

3. The investigation of white-collar crimes requires _____, imagination, the willingness to ask for _____ from other agencies, and increasingly sophisticated computer and technology skills.

4. Frequently, white-collar crime _____ and law enforcement are left in the hands of corporations themselves.

Computer Crime

1. When computers first began emerging in the 1940s, most were complex, large (sometimes filling an entire _____), and difficult, if not _____, for the average person to operate.

2. Today, with the _____ in menu- and icon-driven user-friendly programs, the ease of computer use has made great leaps.

3. For many types of _____ crimes, all one needs is a personal computer (PC) equipped with a modem, the right software, and the desire to commit a crime.

4. Telecommunications crimes generally involve illegal access to or use of computer systems over _____ lines.

5. Computer programs are an aid not only to legitimate businesses, but to _____ ones as well.

Investigating Computer Crime

1. When a report of a computer crime is received by a police _____, the department's report policy is initially followed.

2. Because evidence in computer crime investigations may be electronic records, which are easily lost or

   _____ in error, it is critical that investigators move cautiously.

3. Seizing a computer as _____ must be undertaken very carefully.

Concept Review

For each statement, write **T** *in the space provided if the entire statement is true. Write* **F** *if any part of the statement is false.*

_____ 1. White-collar crimes are equivalent to bunco and confidence games.

_____ 2. The enforcement of laws concerning white-collar offenses is identical to traditional law enforcement.

_____ 3. Historically, law enforcement has virtually ignored many aspects of white-collar crime.

_____ 4. Occupational and corporate crime are two major categories of white-collar crime.

_____ 5. Some forms of white-collar crime rely on the victim's not being able to recognize that he or she is being deceived.

_____ 6. Concealment refers to hiding by white-collar criminals while committing their crimes.

_____ 7. Embezzlement is accomplished only by people in top positions in an organization or business.

_____ 8. Insider trading is actually not a form of white-collar crime, but a form of robbery.

_____ 9. Payola was a serious problem in the music industry during the 1950s and 1960s.

_____ 10. Tax evasion is perhaps the most common form of white-collar crime.

_____ 11. Like many aspects of white-collar criminality, corporate violations are usually policed by various regulatory agencies.

_____ 12. The FBI determines which corporate criminals will be prosecuted and how.

_____ 13. When computers first appeared in the United States, they were large and complex machines.

_____ 14. For most types of computer crimes, one needs expensive and complicated equipment and software.

_____ 15. Computer viruses are a form of internal computer crime.

Key Terms Review

Match the terms with the definitions. Write the letter of the term in the answer column.

a. computer crime
b. insider trading
c. embezzlement
d. white-collar crime
e. hacker
f. payoff
g. computer virus

h. occupational crime
i. industrial espionage
j. kickback
k. payola
l. pick program
m. corporate crime
n. bribe

_____ 1. A nonviolent crime committed by an individual or a corporation that is a breach of trust, confidence, or duty.

_____ 2. The use of one's occupation to illegally obtain personal gain.

_____ 3. Any activity that is undertaken by a corporation for its benefit but violates the law.

_____ 4. The misappropriation or misapplication of money or property entrusted to one's care, custody, or control.

_____ 5. Espionage work undertaken in corporate and industrial areas to keep up with or surpass competitors.

_____ 6. An employee's or manager's use of information gained in the course of his or her job and not generally available to the public to benefit from fluctuations in the stock market.

_____ 7. The payment of cash, goods, or services to someone in exchange for some special service, product, or behavior.

_____ 8. The payment back of a portion of the purchase price to the buyer or public official by the seller to induce a purchase or to improperly influence future purchases.

_____ 9. The receiving of compensation or money from an individual in exchange for some favor.

_____ 10. A payment to a disc jockey for a favor, such as promoting a favorite recording.

_____ 11. A crime committed with or against computers.

_____ 12. A computer program, usually hidden within another computer program, that inserts itself into programs and applications and destroys data or halts execution of programs.

_____ 13. A computer program designed to bypass security measures against duplication of electronic files.

_____ 14. A person who is proficient at using or programming a computer.

Applying Concepts

Determine whether each of the following descriptions is an example of a white-collar crime. Explain your answer.

1. A local convenience store has a petty cash box kept in a drawer under the cash register. A constant total of $100 is kept in the box. When someone uses some of the money, he or she must write the amount used on a summary slip, also kept in the box. Randy Johnson, a clerk employed by the store, uses $10 to pay for a COD delivery, but fails to write the amount on the slip.

   Later, the manager of the store finds the discrepancy in the money and confronts Johnson. Johnson explains what happened, but the manager fires him for stealing.

   _____

   _____

   _____

   _____

   _____

   _____

   _____

   _____

   _____

   _____

   _____

   _____

   _____

   _____

2. A student worker in the dean's office regularly uses the dean's Xerox machine to copy papers for her classes, in spite of a sign over the machine that says, No non-office-related copying allowed.

   _____

   _____

   _____

   _____

3. Katherine Lorraine is the comptroller of a small tool and die company. Among her other responsibilities, she is in charge of the payroll each week. When she pays the employees, she also makes out a check for a phony worker. The check is deposited in a special personnel account bearing her name and that of the company's president. The funds are later divided between Katherine Lorraine and William Bender, the company owner and president.

CHAPTER 21   Narcotics and Dangerous Drugs

Study Outline

Narcotics

1. At one time, the term *narcotic* referred to a variety of substances inducing altered states of consciousness and derived from distillations of the opium _____ plant.

2. Pharmacologically, the designation of _____ remains quite straightforward and specific.

3. The drugs that can be accurately labeled narcotics are limited to two specific categories:

   a. _____

   b. _____

4. When deprived of morphine or heroin, an addict usually experiences the first withdrawal _____ shortly before the time of the next scheduled dose, or _____.

5. Sedatives are used to allay irritation or _____.

6. Hallucinogens are _____ or substances capable of altering perceptions and producing hallucinations.

Types of Narcotics

1. Heroin is an odorless, crystalline white _____.

2. Heroin is not well absorbed if taken _____.

3. Criminal investigators should be aware that many heroin addicts are predatory _____.

4. Cocaine, made from the _____ plant, is a white, odorless, crystalline powder resembling snow, Epsom salts, or camphor.

5. The effects of cocaine include stimulation of the central nervous system and increases in heart _____.

6. Crack cocaine, contrary to popular belief, is neither freebase cocaine nor purified _____.

7. Morphine is the principal alkaloid of _____.

Other Dangerous Drugs

1. Drugs classified as stimulants directly stimulate the central nervous _____.

2. The barbiturates, made from _____ acid, constitute the largest group of sedatives.

3. Tranquilizers were originally developed as medical aids to psychotherapy for _____ patients.

4. Phencyclidine—or, as it is commonly called, PCP—was originally produced as an animal

   _____ and anesthetic.

5. Although sometimes considered a mild hallucinogen, cannabis should actually be put into its own

   _____ .

6. Hashish, or hash, consists of the THC-rich resin scraped from the leaves and _____ of the marijuana plant.

7. Designer drugs are so called because they are created in the _____ by adding or taking away something in an existing drug's chemical composition.

8. Along similar lines to the designer drugs is smokable methamphetamine, or _____.

9. Though not generally considered part of the illicit _____ trade, inhalants have been a serious problem for many law enforcement agencies.

Legal Aspects

1. Federal and _____ laws define drug offenses.

2. Generally, federal and state drug offenses fall into three categories, possession, distribution, and

   _____ of dangerous and/or illicit drugs.

3. Major initiatives against _____ abuse on the federal level were undertaken in the 1980s.

Investigating Illegal Drug Cases

1. Illicit drug cases require special knowledge and familiarity with _____ and other dangerous drugs and their applicable laws.

2. The term *undercover* has been used as a generic label for decoy work, sting operations, and police

   _____-gathering efforts.

3. The use of informants to obtain information, leads, or evidence in police work is common

   _____ .

4. Drug investigators must have a clear understanding of the laws regarding illicit _____, particularly search and seizure laws.

5. There is no special trick to effectively searching persons, property, premises, or _____.

6. The scope of a vehicular search can be better understood by following the rationale set forth in *Chimel*

   v. _____.

7. When patrol officers witness what they believe may be a drug buy, they may not want to immediately

   make an _____.

Concept Review

*For each statement, write **T** in the space provided if the entire statement is true. Write **F** if any part of the statement is false.*

_____ 1. The term *narcotics* technically refers to all mind-altering substances.

_____ 2. Some narcotics are synthetic.

_____ 3. Narcotics have been abused only during the past 50 years.

_____ 4. When deprived of morphine or heroin, an addict usually begins to experience symptoms of withdrawal.

_____ 5. Drug addicts usually have good personal grooming and health habits.

_____ 6. Stimulants tend to increase the activity of the tissue in the central nervous system.

_____ 7. Heroin is typically a colorless, odorless liquid.

_____ 8. Heroin usually arrives in the United States 100 percent pure.

_____ 9. Cocaine derives from the same plant as cocoa beans, which are used to make chocolate.

_____ 10. Cocaine depresses the central nervous system.

_____ 11. Freebasing cocaine can be accomplished in a person's kitchen.

_____ 12. Codeine can be found in some cough medicines.

_____ 13. Barbiturates often are obtained through legitimate channels but are then abused.

_____ 14. Ruffys are really a kind of tranquilizer.

_____ 15. Angel dust is a street name for phencyclidine (PCP).

_____ 16. Another name for mescaline is "magic mushrooms" or "shrooms."

_____ **17.** Marijuana, hash, and hash oil all derive from the cannabis plant.

_____ **18.** The active ingredient in cannabis is called THC.

_____ **19.** Marijuana is highly addictive physically.

_____ **20.** During a light-cover investigation, the investigating officer goes home every evening.

Key Terms Review

Match the terms with the definitions. Write the letter of the term in the answer column.

a. opiate   **h.** light cover
b. probable cause **i.** sedative
c. controlled substance **j.** possession
d. designer drug   **k.** deep cover
e. narcotic   **l.** hallucinogen
f. distribution   **m.** manufacturing
g. stimulant

_____ **1.** Any drug that produces a stupor, insensibility, or sleep.

_____ **2.** Any of the narcotic drugs produced from the opium poppy.

_____ **3.** A drug used to allay irritation or nervousness; creates a lethargy in the user, but may also produce a general feeling of calm and well-being.

_____ **4.** A drug with a stimulating effect on the central nervous system, causing wakefulness and alertness while masking symptoms of fatigue.

_____ **5.** A drug causing changes in sensory perception to create mind-altering hallucinations and loss of an accurate sense of time and space.

_____ **6.** A substance produced in clandestine laboratories by adding or taking away something in an existing drug's chemical composition.

_____ **7.** A drug offense that consists of having a controlled drug on one's person or under one's control, as in one's house or vehicle.

_____ **8.** A drug offense that consists of selling, trading, giving, or delivering illicit drugs, regardless of whether one stands to profit from the transaction.

_____ **9.** A drug offense that includes any activity to cultivate, harvest, produce, process, or manufacture illegal drugs.

_____ **10.** A drug or substance whose use and possession are regulated under the Controlled Substances Act.

_____ **11.** An undercover police operation that extends only as long as the officer's tour of duty.

_____ **12.** An undercover operation that may extend for a long period of time, during which the officer totally assumes another identity.

_____ **13.** Reasonable grounds for belief that a person should be arrested or searched or that a person's property should be searched or seized.

Applying Concepts

Read the description of events that follows. Then answer the questions.

Officers Newson and Novella were on patrol when they saw a man leaning into another man's car at the corner of Maple Street and Fourth Street. Officer Newson recognized the man outside the car as Harris Conners, a petty thief and drug addict. The officers pulled in behind the stopped car. As they did so, Conners looked up, dropped something on the ground, and began to walk north on Maple Street.

Officer Newson called to Conners and ordered him to stop. Conners broke into a run, and Newson took chase on foot. He captured Conners about halfway down the block.

When Officer Newson returned to the car with Conners, he found Officer Novella holding two $20 bills and a small vial of what appeared to be crack cocaine. Officer Novella stated, "I found the vial on the ground here by the car window. It must be what Conners dropped as we drove up. The money was still on the driver's lap."

Conners immediately denied that the drugs were his. The driver of the car, Milton Jones, laughed and said, "You full of shit man. They got us, and I just sold you that junk. They got us dead-bang, so just give it up." In spite of this statement, Conners maintained his innocence. Both men were arrested and advised of their rights.

A search of the vehicle uncovered five more vials of crack cocaine, 2 ounces of marijuana, and $275.

1. Did the officers have probable cause for a search?

_____

_____

_____

_____

_____

_____

_____

_____

_____

_____

_____

_____

_____

_____

2. What charges might be made against the suspects?

_____

_____

_____

_____

_____

_____

_____

_____

3. Can statements made by the suspects be used against them in court?

_____

_____

_____

_____

_____

_____

_____

_____

4. Should the officers have made the arrest? Explain.

_____

_____

_____

_____

_____

_____

_____

_____

CHAPTER 22   Terrorism

Study Outline

Terrorism in Perspective

1. From a law enforcement perspective, *terrorism* is a rather elusive term to accurately define and

   _____.

2. There are a variety of ways _____ might be defined.

3. Political terrorists differ from other types of _____.

Terrorism in the United States

1. Until recently, many Americans did not view political terrorism as a serious threat to safety in the

   _____ States.

2. During the late 1980s and early 1990s, terrorist incidents were witnessed at abortion clinics across the

   United States, as were incidents involving self-styled patriot _____.

Domestic Terrorist Groups

1. The face of domestic terrorism began to change in the mid-_____.

2. There was a decline in traditional _____-_____ extremism and an increase in activities among extremists associated with right-wing groups and special-interest organizations.

3. The most militant of the right-wing groups are the citizen _____ and patriot groups, who continue to attract supporters.

4. Foreign terrorists view the United States as a high-priority _____, an attractive refuge

   from prosecution, and a staging area for obtaining funds and support for their _____.

Legal Aspects of Terrorism

1. The federal government has taken the lead in _____ terrorism.

2. Since 1984, INTERPOL, an _____ policing agency, has had a special group, the Provisional Terrorism Unit, that brings law enforcement skills and authority to international terrorism investigations.

3. Many states include in their charges the offense of _____ threats.

Antiterrorism Activities

1. Among other antiterrorism strategies used by the United States government is its tireless effort to gather _____.

2. Counterintelligence involves obtaining _____ about potential terrorist activities while they are still being planned.

3. Speaking generally, investigating terrorist activities requires techniques similar to those used in investigating organized _____ groups.

Local Police and Terrorism

1. Once a terrorist act has occurred, a patrol unit from the local police is likely to _____ first on the scene.

2. As in other criminal cases, crimes of terrorism require careful and accurate record _____.

3. When officers arrive at the scene of terroristic activity, they may not immediately realize that it is not a _____ crime.

4. History demonstrates that persons involved in terrorism often have previous _____ violations.

5. In addition to items that may have been touched or accidentally left by the terrorist, materials used in bombs or devices may offer _____.

Concept Review

For each statement, write **T** *in the space provided if the entire statement is true. Write* **F** *if any part of the statement is false.*

_____ 1. Terrorism is usually thought to be a crime with political overtones.

_____ 2. Political terrorists differ from other types of criminals.

_____ 3. Before the World Trade Center bombing in New York City, most Americans gave little thought to domestic terrorism.

_____ 4. Throughout the 1970s, police confronted an assortment of domestic American terrorist groups.

_____ 5. Modern-day right-wing groups are extremely conservative groups very distrustful of government activities.

_____ 6. The United States has never been resented in other countries.

_____ 7. INTERPOL's sole responsibility is dealing with international terrorist activities.

_____ 8. A primary effort in antiterrorism is the gathering of counterintelligence.

_____ 9. Local police are never involved in suppression of terroristic activities.

_____ 10. Crimes of terrorism, like more conventional crimes, require accurate and complete record keeping.

_____ 11. Sometimes, when officers first arrive on the scene of a terroristic crime, they believe it is a conventional crime.

_____ 12. Most terrorists have previous criminal backgrounds.

_____ 13. Physical evidence is a critical factor in the identification and location of suspects in cases of terrorism.

_____ 14. Items found at the scene of the terrorism may have been touched or left behind by the terrorist.

_____ 15. Searches of terrorist crime scenes should be confined to the immediate area where the terrorist or terrorists spent most of their time.

Key Terms Review

Match the terms with the definitions. Write the letter of the term in the answer column.

a. international terrorism
b. terrorism
c. suspected terrorist incident
d. crisis negotiation team
e. terroristic threat
f. hate group

g. survivalist training
h. terrorist incident
i. domestic terrorism
j. INTERPOL
k. terrorism prevention
l. counterintelligence

_____ 1. The unlawful use or threat of violence against persons and property to further political or social objectives. It is generally intended to intimidate or coerce a government, individuals, or groups to modify their behavior or policies.

_____ 2. A group antagonistic toward various minority groups in the United States.

_____ 3. An unlawful violent act directed at elements of the U.S. government or population by groups or individuals who are based and operate entirely within the United States and Puerto Rico without foreign direction.

_____ 4. A violent act, or an act dangerous to human life, in violation of the criminal laws of the United States or of any state, to intimidate or coerce a government, the civilian population, or any segment thereof, in furtherance of political or social objectives.

_____ 5. A potential act of terrorism in which responsibility for the act cannot be attributed at the time to a known or suspected terrorist group or individual.

_____ 6. A documented instance in which a violent act by a known or suspected terrorist group or individual with the means and a proven propensity for violence is successfully interdicted through investigative activity.

_____ 7. A type of training in which separatist groups practice guerrilla warfare tactics to prepare to protect themselves from law enforcement officials or other agents of the government.

_____ 8. An unlawful use of force or violence by a group or individual who has some connection to a foreign power or whose activities transcend national boundaries, against persons or property to intimidate or coerce a government or the civilian population to further political or social objectives.

_____ 9. An intergovernmental organization of law enforcement authorities from about 200 countries. Its official name is the International Criminal Police Organization. It works to ensure and promote cooperation and mutual assistance among members.

_____ 10. The unlawful threat of injury or death to manipulate an individual into doing something.

_____ 11. The activity of gathering political and military information about foreign countries and institutions to prevent terrorist attacks.

_____ 12. A group of specialists trained to defuse potentially dangerous situations.

Applying Concepts

Consider the information set forth in the following problem. Describe the actions you would take, given the problem's conditions and situations. Of course, you would notify headquarters. However, what else would you do to save lives and protect property? For example, exactly how would you get the people out of the store without causing panic? What else would have to be done?

At 1600 hours on a busy Saturday, the manager of the Sears department store in the Smallville mall received a package wrapped in plain brown wrapping paper. On the outside was a bright green envelope with the manager's name, Helen Johnson, printed by hand. Johnson opened and read the letter, which stated:

> There is a bomb in this box. It will go off if you try to open it. I am watching you, and if you call the police, I will detonate it by radio control. If you do not want to be responsible for killing hundreds of people in this store, you will do as you are told. We are demanding that you place $10,000 in a shopping bag and leave it on the perfume counter in one hour. We know that you have not yet made a bank deposit for the day and that you should have at least that amount in the store vault by now. If you meet our demands, you and the others in the store will live. If you fail to obey—well, blood and death will be on your hands!

It had been a very busy day at the store, and Johnson knew that the vault held at least the $10,000 demanded. She wondered how the bomber knew so much about the way the store did business. Thinking quickly, she scribbled a note and passed it with the bomber's note to an undercover security officer. She then went to her office to prepare the money. Her note read, "Read the letter and then call the police. I will be in my office readying things."

About ten minutes later, two plainclothes officers arrived at the store, looking for the manager.

_____

_____

_____

_____

_____

_____

CAREER DEVELOPMENT

When someone in a crowd says he or she has a degree in criminal justice or criminology, someone else always asks, "Oh, are you going to be a police officer?" Yet, although being an officer of the law is a noble career choice, job opportunities in these fields are far from being limited to that one. Investigation plays an important role in a wide assortment of careers besides working for a county sheriff's office or a local police department.

Most colleges and universities have career planning or placement centers that typically work with students to explore interests and career options. Unfortunately, in many cases, these job placement centers are geared toward locating jobs for business majors and perhaps liberal arts majors. Often they are inadequate for assisting students interested in criminal justice and criminology careers. This inadequacy places a greater burden on the student. This section will provide some guidance, but it should not be viewed as a complete guide in itself.

The first place to begin a consideration of career choices is with your faculty advisor. As a criminal justice or criminology professor, your advisor is likely to have some good ideas about possible career choices. Many academics maintain contacts with practitioners in the criminal justice field. At the very least, these contacts can help the confused student to better understand certain roles and job opportunities.

Many schools offer internships. These can be very useful to a student who is not entirely certain about a career choice. It is not difficult to spend one semester doing something you thought you might enjoy but soon learn you do not. It is also a fine way to find out if you need any extra course work before graduating. For example, students have discovered, during internships with juvenile delinquency detention centers, that some background in counseling would be very useful. Others have learned, while spending internships with the U.S. Marshal's Service, that some knowledge of bookkeeping and accounting would come in handy. Even students who have undertaken internships with police agencies have come back to campus anxious to take a sociology course on the family or an anthropology course on certain cultures. Internships can be very useful for deciding about careers. They should not be underestimated.

It is very important to recognize, when thinking about a career choice, that this may be what you will be doing for the next 20 or 30 years. Choose something that you believe will be interesting and enjoyable. You probably know at least one person who hates his or her job and lives from vacation to vacation. Many people dislike their jobs so much that they cannot wait for the weekend to roll around. They frequently call in sick. To rationalize keeping such a job, a person may point out that the job pays well or that others would kill to have it—but the person is still unhappy. Other people find themselves stuck in jobs that are going nowhere. Now is the time to make some strategic choices. Therefore, it is time to consider some important questions:

1. What do you really want to do when you finish school?
2. How much additional education are you willing to undertake?
3. What financial rewards do you want, and how much can you expect?
4. Where will this job place you in five years?
5. How can you learn more about the position and its requirements?
6. Do you have the requisite skills for the job?

The first question, "What do you really want to do when you finish school?" is one many good advisors ask students who come seeking advice about careers. Notice, the question is not what do you want to *be,* but what do you want to *do.* One way to consider this is to make a list of at least 10 activities you really like doing. These may include shooting a gun, canoeing down streams, baking cherry pies, playing basketball or other sports, or any other activity. Once you have established what you enjoy *doing,* you and your advisor can figure out which criminal justice careers would let you pursue your activity choices. For example, numerous job opportunities in delinquency work would allow you to play sports with youths, to cook and show children how to cook, and even to go canoeing. By linking career choices to activities you like, you are much more likely to find a career you will enjoy.

The second question, "How much additional education are you willing to undertake?" is important to consider. A number of careers that require only two years of college or perhaps a baccalaureate for an entry-level position require a masters degree for advancement. Learning about educational requirements now, rather than in five years, could make a big difference in your overall career choice. Similarly, you may not have the minimum educational background for certain positions, even though you have a degree. For example, the investigative/enforcement side of the Internal Revenue Service (not the accounting side) requires 15 to 24 credits in accounting. Similarly, postal inspectors must have about 15 credits in accounting for entry-level positions. For many students, these requirements might mean staying in school an extra semester. For others, it might mean selecting a different career.

The third question, "What financial rewards do you want, and how much can you expect?" is intended to be realistic. Many students understand that certain types of jobs pay more or less than others. What some students do not understand is that the cost of living in certain geographic areas also affects salary. For instance, an entry-level probation officer in Erie, Pennsylvania, makes considerably less than an entry-level probation officer in New York City. However, the cost of living and, for many, the quality of life in one location are very different from the other. Therefore, one should not simply set an arbitrary absolute dollar amount as a minimum salary.

The fourth question, "Where will this job place you in five years?" is intended to have you think about career direction. Will this be a dead-end job with little or no possibility of advancement? Or can it be a stepping stone to a better, more interesting, and/or more expansive career? For instance, many of the federal law enforcement agencies require agents to move around quite a bit during the first five years of their careers as operatives. However, after that, there are frequently administrative paths or specializations that allow federal agents to settle into a city for a longer period. In addition, it is not uncommon for an agent from one federal bureau to make a horizontal transfer to another federal bureau after about five years of service.

The fifth question, "How can you learn more about the position and its requirements?" is actually rather easy to answer. Once you have identified several possible career choices, simply contact each agency. Most large agencies have a personnel director or officer. Usually, with a simple telephone call, you can request information about the agency and an application. You can also ask if there are any required tests and, if so, how to register for the next exam.

The final question is "Do you have the requisite skills for the job?" Requisite skills should not be confused or limited to the formal requirement of certain courses or degree majors. Rather, you must answer honestly the question "Can I do this job?" There is no shame in realizing that there are certain tasks you simply cannot bring yourself to undertake. It is far better to realize that now than it would be to recognize it three months or a year into a job.

Once you have considered these six questions, you might also want to consider the following list of related factors. As you read through these work-related elements, rank them in order of how important they actually are to you. Rank them 1 through 15 in descending order, where 1 is the most important to you and 15 is the least important.

———— Amount of salary you receive.

———— Amount of personal freedom you have on the job.

———— Amount of supervision you have over others.

_____ The geographic location of the job.

_____ Your chances for advancement.

_____ Your chance to accomplish something meaningful.

_____ Your sense of self-worth from working at the job.

_____ Your opportunities to improve your education.

_____ Your chances to learn new skills.

_____ Being inside for most of the working day.

_____ Being outside for most of the working day.

_____ How friendly others on the job are.

_____ How professional others on the job are.

_____ The respect others have for the particular career choice.

_____ Your family's view of your job.

By reviewing how you have ranked these 15 elements of working, you may reveal some interesting things about yourself. Consider this newfound information when choosing your career.

Career Opportunities

There are many career opportunities in the areas of criminal justice and criminology. Following is a summary of some of the major types of jobs related, either directly or indirectly, to criminal investigation.

Law Enforcement

The obvious place to begin is in the general area of law enforcement. As the textbook repeatedly indicates, even patrol officers undertake many aspects of criminal investigations. Criminal investigation should be viewed as a partnership between the patrol units and the detectives. In smaller departments, patrol officers are, for all intents and purposes, the investigators. Jobs available at local and state levels include the following:

Police Officer: Uniformed officer who protects the lives and property of the public. Police officers prevent and deter crimes, enforce laws, arrest violators, and render assistance during accidents or crises.

Deputy Sheriff: Uniformed law enforcement position, similar to a police officer. In most Northern states, the sheriff's department may also be responsible for court security and corrections at the county level. In many Southern states, the sheriff's department is the chief law enforcement and investigative agency.

County Constable or County Detective (not available in all communities): Nonuniformed peace officer who frequently works with the local prosecuting attorney's office and hand in hand with local police officers. County constables or county detectives are often found in communities where the police agencies do not have sufficient personnel to staff detective units or where there are no other investigators for the prosecutor's office.

Investigator for the Office of the Public Defender: Nonuniformed investigator found in many larger cities. Such an investigator conducts investigations, interviews witnesses and defendants, and in general helps the public defenders develop their cases.

Investigator for the Office of the Prosecutor: Nonuniformed investigator who serves as the counterpart of the public defender's investigator.

Investigator for the Office of the State Attorney General: These investigators are frequently involved in undercover operations designed to secure evidence against persons involved in illegal activities.

State Police Officer/Trooper (predominantly found in Northeastern states): Uniformed officer entrusted with ensuring public safety and patrolling the interstate highways. In many jurisdictions in the North, the state police are also responsible for forensic tests for the state.

Highway Patrol Officer (predominantly found in the Southern and Southwestern states): Uniformed officer charged with the responsibility of maintaining safety on the highways.

State Regulatory Agency Investigator: There are a number of regulatory agencies who employ people to undertake investigations. These agencies differ in states across the country. Examples of these include state liquor and gambling control boards, fish and wildlife agencies, environmental protection agencies, state alcohol and tobacco agencies, and various types of marine or river patrols.

State Fire Marshal: Designated state fire marshals investigate suspicious and incendiary fires. In addition, marshals are usually called in when there is a fire fatality or when there is a large sum of insurance involved in a fire claim.

At the federal level, jobs related to investigations include the following:

Alcohol, Tobacco and Firearms Special Agent: An ATF agent enforces federal laws regarding firearms, explosives, liquor, and tobacco.

Customs Special Agent: Customs agents are stationed primarily at ports of entry to the United States. Agents may be uniformed or nonuniformed. They investigate frauds against customs revenue and the smuggling of merchandise and contraband into or out of the United States.

Deputy U.S. Marshal: The primary functions of most deputy marshals are more enforcement than investigative. They are responsible for (1) administering the federal witness protection and relocation program; (2) seizing property in both criminal and civil matters to satisfy judgments issued by a federal court; (3) providing security for United States courtrooms and protection to federal judges, jurors, attorneys, and witnesses; and (4) guarding federal prisoners and transporting them to federal institutions when they are transferred or sentenced by a federal court.

Drug Enforcement Agent: Agents of the DEA seek to stop the flow of drugs at their source, both domestic and foreign. Both investigative and enforcement activities are central for agents. Agents may assist in state and local police cases that involve keeping drugs from reaching local communities. Agents are frequently involved in surveillance, undercover operations, raids, interviews of witnesses and suspects, and searches for evidence and contraband.

Federal Bureau of Investigations Special Agent: The FBI is the primary investigative agency of the federal government. Thus, FBI agents are extensively involved in various criminal investigative tasks. The FBI's special agents have jurisdiction over more than 200 federal crimes. Agents are responsible for investigations of both criminal and civil matters and for domestic intelligence dealing with internal security for the nation.

Federal Bureau of Prisons Personnel: Although not extensively involved in criminal investigations, personnel at the Bureau of Prisons are responsible for the care and custody of federal criminals. Bureau personnel plan and execute various research programs to evaluate treatment and rehabilitation programs used by federal correctional institutions.

Immigration and Naturalization Service, Border Patrol Agent: Border patrol agents conduct investigations, detect violations of immigration and naturalization laws, and determine whether aliens may enter or remain in the United States.

Internal Revenue Service, Investigator: The internal revenue investigator is the enforcement agent of the IRS. Agents investigate willful tax evasion, tax fraud, and the money-laundering activities of gamblers and drug dealers.

Postal Inspector: Postal inspectors enforce federal laws pertaining to regulation of mail in the United States. These include laws prohibiting the mailing of explosives, illegal narcotics, obscene material, or articles likely to injure or cause damage. Postal inspectors conduct investigations of mail and mailers of illegal materials. They are also responsible for investigating frauds perpetrated through the mail, such as various Ponzi scams, chain letters, and false prize claims.

Secret Service Agent: Agents have two principal law enforcement functions: to suppress counterfeiting and to suppress forgery of government checks and bonds. The Secret Service is also responsible for the protection of the President of the United States, the President's family members, the President-elect, and the Vice President. The uniformed branch of the Secret Service is also responsible for protecting the White House, the Capitol, and other federal government buildings in Washington, D.C.

The Private Sector

In addition to law enforcement opportunities in the public sector of our society, there are also a number of investigative career opportunities in the private sector. These include the following:

Contract Security Officer: Many firms employ uniformed or nonuniformed guards to work in office buildings, banks, amusement parks, hospitals, and so forth. These guards may be armed or unarmed. Administrative security positions frequently require prior experience as a security guard.

Administrative (Supervisory) Security Positions: These positions involve directing security forces or supervising lower-level security operatives. These positions, like contract guard positions, may exist in large department stores, hotels, hospitals, colleges, amusement parks, and so forth.

Insurance Adjuster/Investigator: Most large insurance companies employ a staff of adjuster/investigators. Their duties include investigating insurance frauds, conducting surveillance, and detecting phony claims.

Private Investigator: *Private investigation* is a catchall term that conjures images of Jim Rockford and Magnum, P.I., and other celebrated television sleuths. However, in the real world, many private investigation firms provide undercover security to supermarkets, retail chains, warehouses, and factories. While private investigations are seldom as glamorous as television might have one believe, they require many investigative skills.

Information Sources on Careers

There are a number of resources students may turn to for information about career and job opportunities in the field of criminal justice and criminology. These sources include the following publications:

ACJS Today
Academy of Criminal Justice Science
Northern Kentucky University
402 Nunn Hall
Highland Heights, KY 41076

The Criminologist
American Society of Criminology
1314 Kinnear Rd., Suite 212
Columbus, OH 43212

DeLucia, Robert C., and Thomas J. Doyle
Career Planning in Criminal Justice
Cincinnati: Anderson Publishing, 1990

Directory of Law Enforcement and Criminal Justice Associations and Research Centers
Law Enforcement Standards Laboratory
National Institute of Standards and Technology
Department of Commerce
Gaithersburg, MD 20899

Harr, Scott J., and Karen M. Hess
Seeking Employment in Criminal Justice and Related Fields
St. Paul: West Publishing, 1996

Law Enforcement Careers
The Career Press, Inc.
62 Beverly Rd., P.O. Box 34
Hawthorne, NJ 07507

National Employment Listing Service Bulletin
Sam Houston State University
College of Criminal Justice
Huntsville, TX 77341

Opportunities in Law Enforcement and Criminal Justice
VGM Career Horizons, 4255 West Touhy Ave.
Lincolnwood, IL 60646-1975

U.S. Department of Labor, Bureau of Labor Statistics
Occupational Outlook Handbook, 1996–1997 edition
Washington, D.C.: USGPO, 1996

Wright, John W.
The American Almanac of Jobs and Salaries, 1994–1995 edition.
New York: Avon Books, 1993

Attributes of a Successful Application

Once you have selected a career, the next task is getting yourself hired. Seeking employment is not accomplished in a mechanical fashion, nor in a vacuum. It is an interaction between the potential employee and the employer. Employers do not search for employees in the abstract; they are looking for people who can fulfill the job description while bringing distinction to the department, agency, or firm. Impressions, therefore—and especially first impressions—are very important.

If you are fortunate enough to secure an interview, be sure to dress appropriately. Seldom will jeans and a polo shirt be appropriate garb for an interview. As a general rule, being a little overdressed for an interview is usually better than being too casually dressed.

Frequently, the first impression a job applicant makes is on paper, usually in his or her résumé and cover letter to the potential employer. Misspellings and sloppy or handwritten letters set a poor tone. Be sure to carefully edit both your cover letter and your résumé.

The Résumé

Preparing an effective résumé is an important part of the job-seeking process for a recent college graduate. Most readers probably know what a résumé is, in the same way they know what brain surgery is. However, just as most readers would not feel comfortable performing brain surgery, many readers may not know how to go about drafting a résumé.

Generally, a résumé is a brief summary of one's career and qualifications. Résumés are frequently used as a screening device by employers, so it is important that you put your best foot forward in yours. Résumés for people applying for entry-level positions are typically about one or two pages long. If your résumé is longer than that, it probably contains unnecessary material that may obscure important information.

Drafting your résumé involves planning, writing, and editing material that describes you, your attributes, and your qualifications for a position. Some of the items you will want to include in your résumé are:

> Your name, address, and telephone number
> Your career objectives
> Your education
> Work experience related to the job
> Special skills, training, or certifications
> Social and/or school activities
> Professional affiliations
> Honors and/or awards
> References

Your Name, Address, and Telephone Number

Although résumé format varies, somewhere at the top, you should indicate your name, address, and telephone number. This is critical information. If you do not include it, a potential employer has difficulty knowing to whom the rest of the résumé belongs. It also makes it more difficult to get in touch with you. Employers tend to seek the path of least resistance. Make things easy for them! One style of résumé presents this information centered on the top of the page.

For example:

John J. Jones
11111 West Maple Street
Smallville, Michigan 42222

Similarly, each heading is placed centered. In other formats the headings and information are all flush left. You can choose the style and format you like best. However, each heading should be all in capital letters and in bold type.

Your Career Objectives

This section is usually suggested as an optional brief statement (perhaps two brief sentences). If you choose to include this, it should be a general statement about the type of position you are seeking. For example:

OBJECTIVE

To obtain a position with a federal agency as an investigator.

Another example:

OBJECTIVE: To secure an investigative position.

Your Education

This section of your résumé should be arranged chronologically, starting with your most recent or highest degree. You should include the type of degree earned, your major, the year your degree was awarded, and the institution issuing the degree. For example:

EDUCATION

B.A.   Criminal Justice, Eastern Kentucky University, 1997.
A.A.   Criminal Justice, Allegheny Community College, 1995.

Work Experience Related to the Job

This section is generally organized chronologically, starting with your most recent job experience. It may also include related volunteer experiences, such as an internship, provided they relate to the position you are seeking. You should not include such positions as baby-sitter, clerk in a supermarket, or newspaper carrier. The idea is to show what *related* work experience you have had that helps qualify you for the position you are seeking.

You should list the full name of each employer, your job title, the city and state where the job was located, and the duration of your employment. In addition, you should include a brief description of your duties and responsibilities on the job. Highlight any special results or accomplishments. It is usually recommended that you use action verbs to describe your responsibilities and accomplishments, beginning statements with verbs such as *accomplished, created, developed, directed, supervised, established, and operated.* Avoid words such as *I, we,* and *my.* Here is an example:

WORK EXPERIENCE

Bantin Guard Service
4321 Roue Blvd.
Chicago, Illinois 64531

Sergeant:
1994–1995

Supervised six guards on patrol at the Big Top Mall. Created and maintained a fluid form of personnel deployment schedule.

Sears Department Store
222 Chicago Circle
Chicago, Illinois 64531

Store Detective:
1992–1993

Operated as a plainclothes security officer.

Special Skills, Training, or Certifications

In this section, you should indicate any special skills, training, or certifications you possess. These may include being CPR-certified by the Red Cross or having taken a special small-arms course in the military. It may also include computer skills, foreign language abilities, or special licenses.
For example:

SPECIAL SKILLS

Certified Firearms Instructor   Obtained at Fort Bragg, 1994.

Conversant with Spanish   Minored in Spanish in college (18 college credits).

Social and/or School Activities

This section gives the job applicant an opportunity to show possible leadership skills and abilities. If you were the president of your sorority or fraternity, here is where you can tell the employer. If you were an Eagle Scout in Boy Scouts, be sure to list that here. If you held any position in student government, indicate what position you held. The idea here is to allow you to highlight activities that may not be directly related to the job but show good character and/or leadership skills. For example:

SOCIAL AND/OR SCHOOL ACTIVITIES

President of Student Government   Eastern Kentucky University
1995–1997

Treasurer, Alpha Phi Sigma   Eastern Kentucky University
National Criminal Justice Honorary
1995

Professional Affiliations

Here you should list memberships in any professional organizations with which you may be affiliated. For example:

PROFESSIONAL AFFILIATIONS

Student Member   American Society of Criminology
                                        1994 to present

Student Member   Academy of Criminal Justice Sciences
                                        1994 to present

References

One important note on selecting people to write your references. It is *not* a good idea to have a reference who wants you to waive your right to see a copy of the recommendation. Stop and think about it. If the recommendation is a good one, why on earth would the reference not want you to see it? If the recommendation is not going to be a good one, why would you want it? Be polite to references who insist on a waiver, thank them, but tell them you will be seeking a reference elsewhere. Employers who receive weak or negative letters of recommendation form a poor impression of the job candidate. Certainly, such letters do not demonstrate good judgment on the candidate's part.

References can be indicated in at least two ways on the résumé. First, there may be a heading followed by the statement "References will be furnished upon request."

Second, under the heading References, there may be a list that includes the full name, address, and telephone number of each reference. Usually three or four references are listed. References should be sought from people who can speak knowledgeably about your skills and qualifications. If these are past teachers of yours, they should be instructors of courses in which you received good grades. For example:

REFERENCES

Dr. William Savage   Dr. Kenneth Pollack
Department of Criminal Justice   Department of Sociology
Anywhere University   Anywhere University
Smallville, Michigan 42341   Smallville, Michigan 42341
(513) 555-2525   (513) 555-2232

Dr. Judith Anderson-Brown
Department of Criminal Justice
Anywhere University
Smallville, Michigan 42341
(513) 555-2527

Complete sample résumé:

John J. Jones
11111 West Maple Street
Smallville, Michigan 42222

OBJECTIVE

To obtain a position with a federal agency as an investigator.

EDUCATION

B.A.	Criminal Justice, Eastern Kentucky University, 1997.
A.A.	Criminal Justice, Allegheny Community College, 1995.

WORK EXPERIENCE

Bantin Guard Service
4321 Roue Blvd.
Chicago, Illinois 64531

Sergeant:
1994–1995

Supervised six guards on patrol at the Big Top Mall. Created and maintained a fluid form of personnel deployment schedule.

Sears Department Store
222 Chicago Circle
Chicago, Illinois 64531

Store Detective:
1992–1993

Operated as a plainclothes security officer.

SPECIAL SKILLS

Certified Firearms Instructor — Obtained at Fort Bragg, 1994.

Conversant with Spanish — Minored in Spanish in college (18 college credits).

SOCIAL AND/OR SCHOOL ACTIVITIES

President of Student Government, 1995–1997 — Eastern Kentucky University

Treasurer, Alpha Phi Sigma National Criminal Justice Honorary, 1995 — Eastern Kentucky University

PROFESSIONAL AFFILIATIONS

Student Member — American Society of Criminology
1994 to present

Student Member — Academy of Criminal Justice Sciences
1994 to present

REFERENCES

Dr. William Savage
Department of Criminal Justice
Anywhere University
Smallville, Michigan 42341
(513) 555-2525

Dr. Judith Anderson-Brown
Department of Criminal Justice
Anywhere University
Smallville, Michigan 42341
(513) 555-2527

Dr. Kenneth Pollack
Department of Sociology
Anywhere University
Smallville, Michigan 42341
(513) 555-2232

The Cover Letter

You should never send a résumé to a potential employer without accompanying it with a cover letter. Even if you have spoken with the potential employer on the telephone and have been invited to submit a résumé, include a cover letter. Anything less may be viewed as poor initiative on the part of the job candidate.

A cover letter gives the candidate an opportunity to introduce himself or herself to the prospective employer. It should be short and to the point. It should not merely repeat information already shown on the résumé. Rather, it is an opportunity to highlight certain areas of accomplishment that may not be expressed completely on the résumé. The idea of a cover letter should be to entice the potential employer into wanting to find out more about you.

A cover letter should contain certain basic elements, as follows:

1. It should be addressed to a specific person and agency. If the name of the specific person is not known, a title, such as Personnel Officer, Director, or Chief—whatever is appropriate for that employer—can be substituted. However, a quick telephone call to the agency will usually secure the name of the person you should be writing to.

2. Cover letters should begin with an explanation of why you are writing, such as, "Your opening for the position of Insurance Investigator is of great interest to me."

3. Tell how you heard about the position. For instance, "I learned about this position from an advertisement in the *National Employment Listing Service Bulletin.*"

4. Sell yourself. No employer wants a wishy-washy candidate who basically says, "I want this job, but I don't really know why anyone would want to hire me." Tell the potential employer why he or she *does* want to hire you.

5. Tell the potential employer why you want to work for the agency, company, or organization. If it was a childhood dream to become a police officer, be sure to tell the reader of your cover letter this fact.

6. Never lie or overembellish in a cover letter. Lying in cover letters has a strange way of coming back to haunt the liar. Do not do it!

7. Always indicate a willingness and desire to meet personally with the potential employer for an interview. You should also indicate how you will follow up on your application letter or how the employer may contact you.

8. Finally, always use a cover letter written specifically for the employer to whom you are applying. This is not to say you cannot put a fairly standard letter on your word processor and use it over and over with only minor alterations. But do not write a generic "To Whom It May Concern" letter and photocopy it along with your résumé.

An effective format for a cover letter is block style. In this format, everything begins flush left at the margin. The parts of the cover letter, then, would appear as follows:

Your Name
Your Address
City, State, and Zip Code
Date of Letter

[space]
Name of Addressee
Title of Addressee
Name of the Organization
Full Address of Potential Employer

[space]
Salutation (Dear Chief Johnson:)

[space]
Opening Paragraph: Explanation of why you are writing and how you heard about the position.

[space]
Second Paragraph: Selling yourself. Entice the employer so that he or she will want to meet you. Tell the employer why you want to work for the organization.

[space]
Concluding Paragraph: Indicate a willingness and desire to meet with the prospective employer. Indicate how the employer can best get in touch with you.

[space]
Closing (Sincerely,)

[about 4 spaces (Sign your name in this space.)]

Typed Name

Sample Cover Letter

Ms. Katherine Lawrence
123 Third Street
Buffalo, New York 13456
January 9, 1997

Alex Gerald
Personnel Officer
Buffalo Police Department
2345 Elmwood Avenue
Buffalo, New York 13456

Dear Officer Gerald:

The opening for the position of patrol officer in your department is of interest to me. I heard about this position from Sergeant Edelstein of your department, who is a friend of my father's.

Accompanying this letter is a résumé illustrating my background, qualifications, and previous work experience. Having now completed my baccalaureate in criminal justice, and two summers as a seasonal police officer in Ocean City, Maryland, I am very interested in beginning a career as a full-time officer with the Buffalo Police Department. Throughout my college career at Northwestern University, I looked forward to returning to Buffalo and joining the police department.

I sincerely believe that I can make a strong, positive contribution to the department. I would be delighted to meet with you at your convenience and discuss my candidacy as a police officer. I will call you the week of January 15 to make sure my résumé was received. Perhaps, at that time, we can arrange an interview. I will look forward to speaking with you.

Sincerely,

Katherine Lawrence

The Interview

In addition to cover letters and résumés, interviews provide an important opportunity to make a good impression. Usually, only a very small proportion of applicants will reach the point of interviewing for a position. You need to approach an interview, then, as if you may never receive another chance at this job. Take it seriously, but do not paralyze yourself with concern. Remember, interviews are two-way streets. Not only are you trying to convince the potential employer to hire you, but they should be trying to convince you that you want to join them.

As mentioned previously, it is important to dress appropriately. If you are unaccustomed to dressing up, consult a friend whom you believe dresses well. Or go to a good department store and ask a salesperson what he or she might recommend for an interview. It may take a little time and money to create a good interviewing outfit, but it will be worth it in the long run.

In general, it is better to spend some time wearing your interview outfit—even if only in the house—before going on the interview. You need to feel comfortable during the interview. That comfort sometimes requires breaking in the new clothes. There is nothing more disconcerting for an interviewer than watching an applicant fidgeting with a necktie or rubbing a sore heel caused by a pair of new shoes.

Avoid outlandish styles, bright colors, unnecessary jewelry, and strong-smelling or lavishly applied cologne or perfume. All of these can create undesirable distractions for the interviewer.

It is also important to find out as much as you can about the job and the organization before the interview. You should be able to ask relevant questions and to display at least a general knowledge of the employer. It is always impressive to an interviewer to see that a candidate has done his or her homework about the agency.

It is never bad form to arrive for an interview 5, 10, or even 15 minutes early. It is always bad form to arrive even 2 minutes late! Be aware that you never really know who may be watching or listening. Avoid unflattering chatter about the agency or people in the agency with others who may be waiting for interviews as well. The best advice may be to sit silently, smiling to greet others, but not engaging in conversation.

It is also useful to sharpen your interview skills and to give some thought to answers for questions likely to be asked of you. Following is a list of some of the more common questions asked during job interviews. Knowing how you are going to answer these should help relax you for the more difficult and less predictable kinds of questions that might arise.

- Why do you want to work for us?
- What previous jobs have you held?
- Have you ever been fired from a position? If so, why?
- What sorts of activities were you involved in during high school? During college?
- What can you tell us about our agency?
- Why did you choose the college you attended?
- What was your major, and why?
- Do you like working with other people or alone? Why?
- What was the worst part of your last job?
- What did you learn about yourself from your last job?
- Of all the jobs you have ever held, which one did you like the most? Why?
- What special skill or ability would you say you could contribute to the agency?
- What kind of work interests you?
- Tell me about yourself.
- What would you say is your strongest quality?
- What would you say is your greatest weakness?
- What would you say is your greatest accomplishment?

- Why should we hire you?
- Do you have any questions for us?

You should also prepare several questions of your own to ask the interviewer. Usually, at some point in the interview, the interviewer will ask if you have any questions for him or her. If you have none, this may be taken to mean you have not given very much thought to getting this job. The following is a list of some general questions you should feel comfortable asking an interviewer.

- What is the timetable for filling this position?
- Is there a formal orientation of some sort for new employees?
- How frequently are employees asked to work overtime?
- How does reimbursement work for work-related travel?
- Are there any special programs or projects being undertaken by the agency right now?
- What educational or specialized training programs are supported by the agency or available to employees?
- What is the salary range for the position I have applied for? Who makes the final salary decision?

At the conclusion of an interview, it is a good idea to ask, "Have you any final questions for me?" You might also leave the interviewer with a brief verbal summary of your strengths, why you would be a good hire, and your serious interest in the position. You might also ask what will happen next. Finally, be sure to thank the interviewer for his or her time and to extend your hand to shake the interviewer's. Use a firm, solid handshake that tells the interviewer you have self-confidence.

After an interview, it is always a good idea to send a very brief thank-you letter. Again, address the letter to the interviewer personally. Keep the message short. Thank the interviewer for his or her time, and reinforce your enthusiastic interest in the position.

Sample Thank-You Letter

Ms. Katherine Lawrence
123 Third Street
Buffalo, New York 13456
January 26, 1998

Alex Gerald
Personnel Officer
Buffalo Police Department
2345 Elmwood Avenue
Buffalo, New York 13456

Dear Officer Gerald:

Thank you very much for taking the time to speak with me yesterday about my candidacy for a position as a patrol officer with your department. This position is exactly what I was looking for. I genuinely hope that you will give my application serious consideration. I will look forward to hearing from you again soon.

Sincerely,

Katherine Lawrence

As previously mentioned, a job interview is an opportunity for both the employer and you to look one another over. Before accepting a position, you want to be pretty sure that the job is what you think it will be, and that you will enjoy this type of work. Sometimes, the job seems fine, but the people you will have to work with are simply not your cup of tea. Be aware that accepting or passing on a job is not the end of the world. Should you make a mistake during the interview, learn from the mistake, and try to avoid making it again in the future.

Foremost, during the interview process, remain calm, interested, and enthusiastic. Try at all times to project a positive, self-confident attitude. Even if a question throws you a bit, answer honestly. A simple "Gee, I really never gave that much thought before" is usually better than some half-baked lie.

Good luck in your job search!

Chapter 1

Concept Review

1. F	**6.** T
2. F	**7.** T
3. T	**8.** F
4. F	**9.** F
5. F	**10.** T

Key Terms Review

1. g	**7.** i	**13.** h
2. o	**8.** a	**14.** n
3. d	**9.** m	**15.** b
4. l	**10.** j	**16.** k
5. f	**11.** r	**17.** e
6. p	**12.** c	**18.** q

Applying Concepts

1. **a.** Deduction
   b. Induction
   c. Induction
2. **a.** Although the person standing over the body may be the attacker, it remains to be determined whether the victim was even stabbed. It also remains to be seen whether the knife held by the man is the murder weapon, even if the victim was stabbed. The blood on the knife may not even be human blood. It is important to avoid jumping to conclusions, whether one uses deductive reasoning or inductive.
   b. Although the officer may be inclined to infer that no domestic disturbance has taken place, it is important to establish this as fact. The officer should have separated all four parties and then briefly interviewed each before drawing any conclusion. It may be that the man on the couch is unconscious from a blow to the head, and not simply sleeping. The woman could be washing blood off the frying pan used to hit the man. Or the man may be in an alcoholic stupor after an altercation with his wife or children. Officers should not draw conclusions without investigation.
   c. It is important that when answering crimes-in-progress calls, officers use extreme caution. That caution extends to trusting people already on the scene. The "helpful citizens" directing the officer to the alley may well be the robbers. A better strategy would have been to escort those people back to the store and talk with the merchant.

Chapter 2

Concept Review

1. T	**6.** T	**11.** T	**16.** T
2. T	**7.** T	**12.** F	**17.** F
3. F	**8.** F	**13.** F	**18.** T
4. F	**9.** F	**14.** F	**19.** T
5. F	**10.** T	**15.** T	**20.** F

Key Terms Review

1. d	**7.** e	**12.** f
2. g	**8.** l	**13.** j
3. h	**9.** p	**14.** m
4. a	**10.** c	**15.** b
5. i	**11.** o	**16.** k
6. n		

Applying Concepts

1. The first thing to do is to call for medical assistance for the fallen officer. There is probably little you can do for the officer, unless you have medical training. Therefore, it is probably better to pursue the assailant. After all, anyone who would shoot a police officer is a serious risk to the public. While pursuing the suspect, you should radio in a description of the car and any part of the license plate number you may have seen. Most agencies have policies regarding high-speed pursuits, and you should be aware of these. Follow the suspect at a safe speed and distance. Most agencies have policies against shooting at fleeing felons, and you should also be aware of these. It is important to remember that in any pursuit, other officers will be assisting and you should operate as a team. Eventually, if the suspect does not stop on his or her own or crash, he or she will run out of fuel. At some point, the suspect will have to come to a stop.
2. The major problem here, of course, is that the officers never gave the suspect his *Miranda* warnings. Thus, the fact that he admitted raping both the 11-year-old and her best friend could not be used against him in court. Clearly, by calling him names and repeatedly asking him while he was in custody why he had committed the crime (interrogating him), the officers violated his constitutional rights.

Chapter 3

Concept Review

1. F	**6.** F
2. T	**7.** T
3. F	**8.** T
4. F	**9.** T
5. T	**10.** F

Key Terms Review

1. i	**8.** a
2. e	**9.** k
3. b	**10.** f
4. g	**11.** l
5. m	**12.** c
6. d	**13.** h
7. j	

Applying Concepts

First, the store should be secured and no unauthorized people allowed inside. Next, photographs and sketches should be made of the area. While this is going on, the clerk should be given necessary medical treatment and interviewed.

After completing these activities, the investigating officer should be able to find a number of potentially identifying and incriminating items left at the scene. For example, there should be fingerprints on items in the shopping cart. This is especially true for the Fresca bottle, the *TV Guide,* the package of American cheese, and the bottle of mustard. All of these items have hard, smooth surfaces, where fingerprints could easily be left. Also, the droplets of blood from the suspect should be collected and processed for identification purposes. Blood samples should be obtained from the victim to avoid confusing the blood lost by the victim with that lost by the suspect. In addition, the clerk's clothes should be carefully collected to be examined for fibers and/or hair from the suspect.

The bullets fired by the suspect should be recovered, correctly tagged, and recorded. In addition, a bulletin with a description of the suspect and his vehicle should be broadcast.

Chapter 4

Concept Review

1. F	**6.** F
2. F	**7.** T
3. T	**8.** T
4. F	**9.** T
5. T	**10.** F

Key Terms143

Review

1. g	**6.** a
2. e	**7.** d
3. c	**8.** i
4. j	**9.** f
5. h	**10.** b

Applying Concepts

A number of tests that the police can arrange to have run will give them insight about how viable a suspect Henry is. First, they can determine his blood type. If he is not AB, he is not a very good candidate—assuming the blood under Genie's nails is from the assailant. To further check on Henry, DNA tests can be made of the sperm found in Genie's vagina and of samples from Henry. If he is being truthful about having used a condom, the DNA tests should demonstrate that the sperm is not his. Finally, the police may want to hook Henry up to a polygraph machine to determine how truthfully he answers questions regarding the date, the rape, and the murder.

Chapter 5

Concept Review

1. F	**7.** F
2. T	**8.** T
3. T	**9.** F
4. F	**10.** F
5. T	**11.** T
6. F	**12.** T

Key Terms Review

1. c	**6.** i
2. f	**7.** a
3. h	**8.** j
4. b	**9.** d
5. e	**10.** g

Applying Concepts

1. Cases A, C, and D all have the following similarities: no forced entry; similar burglary times; the taking of only electronic equipment—even when other valuables are present; and what may be a signature, namely, the torn or vandalized items left strewn around the place. These similarities suggest that all three of these burglaries were accomplished by the same burglar or burglars. If you consider the size and weight of some of the items taken, it is possible that more than a single burglar is involved.

   Case B had forced entry, and characteristically different kinds of things were taken. In addition, the burglary was undertaken at a different time from the others, and it did not involve any vandalism. It may even suggest a more professional burglary than the others.

2. Psychological profiles usually begin with a difficult, bizarre, or persistent wave of crime. Such a wave might be represented by a serial killer. A behavioral specialist, often a psychologist or psychiatrist, is asked the basic question "What sort of person would do a thing like this?" After reviewing the facts of the case, and often after a visit to the actual crime scene, the specialist can establish a profile of the kind of person who committed the crime.

   The basic process of psychological profiling is to try to recognize and interpret visible evidence at the scene as indicating certain aspects of the criminal's personality. Profiles are not uniform and do not always produce the same information or results.

Chapter 6

Concept Review

1. F	**6.** F	**11.** F	**16.** T
2. F	**7.** T	**12.** T	**17.** F
3. T	**8.** F	**13.** T	**18.** F
4. T	**9.** F	**14.** F	**19.** T
5. F	**10.** F	**15.** F	**20.** T

Key Terms Review

1. h	**6.** a	**11.** c
2. b	**7.** n	**12.** j
3. k	**8.** f	**13.** g
4. e	**9.** i	**14.** d
5. m	**10.** l	

Applying Concepts

1. During the interview, it is important to obtain a complete description of the suspect and, if possible, of the weapon. Also be sure to determine the contents of the wallet. The interviewer should also ask how the suspect left the area and in which direction. Remember, the idea of this exercise is to give you an opportunity to conduct an interview. There is no absolutely right or wrong way to undertake this activity.

2. Your answer to the preparation question should include the intention of looking over the suspect's criminal history before interrogating him. It should also include reviewing your notes from the interview with the victim. Your questions for the suspect should include an attempt to determine where he was on the day and at the time of the robbery. You should also seek information concerning the gun. If possible, you should plan to ask questions that provide the suspect an opportunity to admit his guilt.

Chapter 7

Concept Review

1. T	**7.** F	**13.** T
2. T	**8.** T	**14.** T
3. F	**9.** T	**15.** T
4. T	**10.** T	**16.** F
5. F	**11.** F	**17.** F
6. F	**12.** T	**18.** F

Key Terms Review

1. c	**6.** k	**11.** i
2. h	**7.** d	**12.** f
3. e	**8.** g	**13.** m
4. j	**9.** l	
5. b	**10.** a	

Apply Concepts

1. There are a number of inexpensive items that could go into a portable fingerprint kit. These include:

   Latex gloves
   A flashlight
   Rolls of cellophane tape (of differing widths)
   Scissors
   Tongs and tweezers
   Fingerprint powder (Graphite and baking powder will suffice.)
   Several small artist's paintbrushes
   Latent-print transfer cards
   A camera with a fixed-focus lens
   A notebook and a pen or pencil

2. Although thumbprints will differ, you should look for the core at the center of the impression. In loops, whorls, and composites, the delta is the ridge formation nearest the center of divergence of two types of lines. Arches are ridges that flow from one side of the impression to the other side with a wave in the center. Loops usually enter from one side of the impression, make a hairpin turn, and exit on the side from which they entered. In whorl patterns, at least one ridge must make a complete curvature about the core or center. This curve—which may be in the form of a spiral, a circle, an oval, or any variant of a circle—makes at least one curve in front of each delta.

Chapter 8

Concept Review

1. F	**6.** T	**11.** F	**16.** T
2. F	**7.** T	**12.** T	**17.** F
3. F	**8.** T	**13.** T	**18.** T
4. T	**9.** F	**14.** F	**19.** T
5. T	**10.** T	**15.** F	**20.** T

Key Terms Review

1. c	**6.** j	
2. h	**7.** a	
3. b	**8.** i	
4. g	**9.** f	
5. e	**10.** d	

Applying Concepts

1. The investigating officer must determine that there is probable cause to warrant a wiretapping. The officer must convince a judge that the information obtained will enhance existing evidence and will provide additional evidence of the suspect's guilt. Wiretaps should not be used capriciously or to gather incriminating evidence where a mere suspicion exists. Such use seriously jeopardizes citizens' rights to privacy.

2. In answering this question, you should be as creative as possible. At a minimum, however, your response should include these major sources of information:

   Asking his cousin.
   Determining where other relatives live (through the cousin).
   Speaking with friends or neighbors (determined from an interview with the cousin).
   Contacting his employer (if already known or learned from the cousin).
   Checking with the U.S. Postal Service for a forwarding address.
   Checking with the phone company and utilities to see where the final bills were sent.
   Checking with the department of motor vehicles to see if he has received any tickets, changed his automobile registration, or updated his driver's license.

   Naturally, your list may include other sources of information.

Chapter 9

Concept Review

1. F	**6.** F	**11.** T	**16.** T
2. T	**7.** T	**12.** T	**17.** F
3. T	**8.** F	**13.** F	**18.** T
4. T	**9.** F	**14.** T	**19.** T
5. F	**10.** T	**15.** T	**20.** F

Key Terms Review

1. c	**5.** a	**9.** d
2. l	**6.** k	**10.** i
3. e	**7.** h	**11.** f
4. g	**8.** j	**12.** b

Applying Concepts

Robbery at the Motel 6

Facts

One possible rewriting of the report is as follows:

On August 13, 1998, at 1130 hours, the proprietor of the Motel 6 at Withville, Virginia, John A. Fisher, was robbed.

The robbery occurred as Fisher was leaving his living quarters at the motel. Fisher states he heard a knock at the door to his apartment, number 8 at the motel. When he opened the door, an unknown white man rushed into the room. The suspect pointed a blue steel revolver at Fisher's head and ordered him to open the wall safe, located behind a print on the wall. Fisher states that the suspect said, "Hurry up. I've been watching you for days. I have nothing to lose if I kill you."

Fisher states he opened the safe and gave the suspect its contents, which included $2500 cash, one man's white gold ring with the initials *JAF* on an onyx setting (valued at $150), and one string of pearls (valued at $800). In addition, Fisher states that the suspect took $185 from a small cigar box under the reception counter. The total estimated loss from this robbery is $3635. Fisher states that he is fully covered for this loss by insurance.

Fisher states that the suspect placed the stolen property and cash in his overcoat pocket. The suspect then ordered Fisher to face the wall and remain there for ten minutes. The suspect warned Fisher that if he did not comply, he would "blow your damn head off." The suspect also said, "I'll be watching you." Fisher states that the suspect then fled through the front door. Fisher remained in the room. About two minutes passed before Fisher heard what he believes was a car speeding away. Fisher was not sure if the car he heard was the suspect's, so he waited three more minutes before phoning the police to report the robbery.

Officers Thomas Novice and Judy Newcop arrived at the scene at 1145 hours and took the following description of the suspect: 5'5" to 5'7", 165–175 pounds, stocky build, 28–30 years old, ruddy complexion, sandy blond hair, and blue eyes.

The suspect was wearing an olive green baseball cap, a black oilcloth duster, dark black cowboy boots with a red S-shaped design on the side, and black leather driving gloves. Fisher could not identify the type of pistol used in the robbery, but stated that the suspect held the pistol in his right hand. Officers Novice and Newcop issued a broadcast of the suspect's description.

In a canvass of the motel, Officers Novice and Newcop could locate no one who had heard or seen anything during the time of the robbery. Fisher was escorted to department headquarters and asked to view the department's mug file for a possible suspect. Fisher was unable to identify anyone.

The investigation will continue.

Chapter 10

Concept Review

1. F	**6.** T	**11.** T
2. F	**7.** T	**12.** T
3. T	**8.** T	**13.** F
4. F	**9.** T	**14.** T
5. F	**10.** F	**15.** T

Key Terms Review

1. e	**7.** g	**13.** f
2. m	**8.** o	**14.** h
3. d	**9.** k	**15.** l
4. p	**10.** b	**16.** a
5. c	**11.** i	
6. j	**12.** n	

Applying Concepts

1. Most departments have formal policies against surrendering your weapon in hostage situations. This is still a difficult decision to make. However, remember that the suspect has threatened to kill your partner. Probably the only thing stopping him from doing that is knowing that once he has lost his hostage, you will shoot him. If you give up your weapon, you may be endangering both your life and your partner's. In addition, other people in the supermarket may also be at risk. Your best choice, therefore, is to try to talk the gunman into realizing the futility of his effort and surrendering himself.

2. In this situation, you have not yet entered the store or been seen by the two robbers. Your best action would be to slip into the next store and have someone there call 911 to report a robbery in progress at the pharmacy. Then you should return to your own car and place it in a position from which you can watch the two robbers without being noticed. If the robbers exit the pharmacy before back-up officers arrive, you should carefully conduct a moving surveillance and should report their location as soon as possible. To enter the pharmacy and attempt any television-style heroics would place the four customers, the proprietor, and you in danger.

Chapter 11

Concept Review

1. F	**6.** T	**11.** T
2. T	**7.** T	**12.** F
3. F	**8.** F	**13.** T
4. T	**9.** F	**14.** T
5. F	**10.** T	**15.** T

Key Terms Review

1. m	**6.** b	**10.** a
2. d	**7.** e	**11.** j
3. h	**8.** i	**12.** c
4. f	**9.** l	**13.** g
5. k		

Applying Concepts

1. **a.** No assault **d.** Aggravated assault
   b. Simple assault **e.** Aggravated assault
   c. Simple assault **f.** No assault

2. **a.** Since the striking of the other boy was an accident, it does not constitute any form of assault.

   b. In this case, Mrs. Richey inappropriately struck the teacher. In some jurisdictions, this would constitute a simple battery; however, most modern statutes would classify it as a simple assault. It is an overt act demonstrating intent and ability to carry out the infliction of bodily harm on another.

   c. As in many simple assaults, this situation is a dispute that escalated to physical violence, which, in this case, amounts to a simple assault.

   d. Janet used an implement—the pool cue—that could be construed as a weapon. Certainly, striking someone over the head with a wooden object will inflict greater bodily harm than slapping the person or striking him or her with a fist. The addition of the weapon turns this assault into an aggravated one.

   e. In this case, Jack intentionally sought to cause bodily harm to his boss but chose to try to make it seem an accident. Not only does Jack have the *mens rea* (intent in mind), but he has also discussed it with another person. Legally, this suggests an aggravated assault, although proving it may require Ted to offer testimony.

   f. The use of force in the course of an officer's attempt to make a lawful arrest does not constitute an assault, unless it can be shown that the force was unnecessary or excessive. In the situation offered, it appears justified.

Chapter 12

Concept Review

1. F	6. F	11. F	16. T
2. F	7. T	12. T	17. T
3. T	8. F	13. T	18. F
4. F	9. T	14. T	19. T
5. T	10. T	15. F	20. T

Key Terms Review

1. b	6. a	11. f
2. g	7. n	12. h
3. e	8. l	13. d
4. i	9. c	14. o
5. k	10. j	15. m

Applying Concepts

Cases like the one described are heart-wrenching. Many people might secretly want to beat the information out of the suspect. This, however, is not an option for you or your partner. Such an action would be criminal and would undermine the foundation of the criminal justice system. However, you may have sufficient information and probable cause to obtain a search warrant for Henderson's home and car. There you may find sufficient evidence to charge him with a crime. In the face of criminal charges, Henderson may become more talkative.

The unfortunate reality of such a case is that you may have to release Henderson. Although you may be able to keep him under close surveillance, it may simply be too little too late for the girl. Sadly, except on television, the police do not always manage to get to the victim in the nick of time.

Chapter 13

Concept Review

1. F	6. F	11. F	16. T
2. F	7. T	12. T	17. F
3. F	8. T	13. T	18. T
4. T	9. T	14. F	19. T
5. F	10. T	15. T	20. F

Key Terms Review

1. b.	5. c
2. f	6. g
3. d	7. e
4. h	8. a

Applying Concepts

The first thing to do is to contact the country club and determine if Somers arrived and if he is still there playing golf. If he is not there and he has still not returned to work or home, he should be considered kidnapped.

Mrs. Somers should be told to begin going through the motions of putting the money together, since the note indicates she is being watched. Investigators in an unmarked car should meet her at her home to discuss the kidnapping. The letter should be taken into custody and a copy made for Mrs. Somers.

The letter should be examined for fingerprints, possible identifying watermarks, print characteristics, and so forth.

A full description of the woman who gave him the note should be obtained from Peter Conrad. He should also view file mug shots to try to identify the woman.

Given the short time allowed, a homing device should be secured in the sports bag, and its transmissions monitored by officers in unmarked cars. The money should be marked to be used as evidence later. The payoff should be undertaken with undercover officers in place to follow the pickup person.

Chapter 14

Concept Review

1. F	**6.** F	**11.** T	**16.** F
2. T	**7.** T	**12.** F	**17.** F
3. T	**8.** T	**13.** F	**18.** F
4. T	**9.** T	**14.** F	**19.** F
5. T	**10.** F	**15.** T	**20.** T

Key Terms Review

1. d	**6.** q	**11.** p	**16.** s
2. m	**7.** h	**12.** g	**17.** f
3. j	**8.** k	**13.** n	**18.** t
4. o	**9.** r	**14.** l	**19.** i
5. a	**10.** b	**15.** c	**20.** e

Applying Concepts

Your answer should include a description of how you would secure the area; what items you would take as evidence (and how you would take them); which forensic or other personnel you would summon, including the coroner; who you would interview; and, in general, how you would find answers to the questions *who, what, where, when, how,* and *why.*

Chapter 15

Concept Review

1. F	**6.** T	**11.** T
2. T	**7.** T	**12.** F
3. F	**8.** T	**13.** F
4. F	**9.** F	**14.** F
5. F	**10.** T	**15.** F

Key Terms Review

1. b	**5.** g
2. f	**6.** h
3. d	**7.** c
4. a	**8.** e

Applying Concepts

1. **a.** Ripping and peeling: This method is used on fire-resistant safes because of their construction. They typically have a lightweight metal outer shell that can be peeled off the door with a bar, exposing the locking mechanism. Alternatively, the side of the safe may be ripped off with pliers and cutting tools. The insulation material can then be chiseled or cut away to gain entry.
   b. Chopping: This is a rather crude way to open a safe. It involves turning the safe upside down and assaulting the bottom with an ax or a sledgehammer. The assault continues until there is a hole large enough to permit the thief's hand to reach inside and take out the contents. Because of the time and noise involved, chopping is sometimes undertaken when the safe can be moved to a secluded location.
   c. Explosives: The use of explosives is not common in safe burglary today. When it is undertaken, it is usually accomplished by several safe burglars working as a team. Each team member usually has a special task to perform.
2. **a.** Burglary during a party: In this type of burglary, a thief burglarizes the bedrooms or other household areas where guests leave their valuables during a party. The burglar may be a guest or may have crashed the party.
   b. Invading burglary: In this type of crime, criminals ring the doorbell and then burst into the home when the door is opened. In some cases, kidnapping and assaults may occur. In other cases, the culprits swiftly take valuables from the home and then flee. A common M.O. in this type of crime during the recent past has been the targeting of Asian victims by Asian criminals.
   c. Window smashing: This type of burglary usually has a commercial target, such as a jewelry store or an electronics store. The basic M.O. associated with this crime is the smashing of a display window and the grabbing of items on display.

Chapter 16

Concept Review

1. T	**6.** F	**11.** T
2. F	**7.** T	**12.** T
3. T	**8.** T	**13.** F
4. T	**9.** T	**14.** F
5. T	**10.** F	**15.** T

Key Terms Review

1. d	**5.** k	**9.** j
2. i	**6.** g	**10.** h
3. f	**7.** b	**11.** a
4. c	**8.** l	**12.** e

Applying Concepts

1. There are no absolutely correct or incorrect answers to this question. Be sure, however, that your answer includes both the obvious types, such as three-card monte and fraudulent check writing, as well as more subtle types, such as various business deceptions. Consider, in your answer, why certain confidence and bunco crimes might be more likely than others to occur in your locale.

2. To avoid fraudulent checks, merchants should be sure to check photographic identification. Unfortunately, bad checks may occur even with the tightest security. However, obtaining sufficient identification information, such as the check writer's correct telephone number and address, may help in securing funds for bad checks. In many areas, merchants may also subscribe to a check assurance company. By calling the company, the merchant can often determine if a check is likely to be bad. Many of these services will also make good on bad checks they have assured.

Chapter 17

Concept Review

1. F	**6.** F	**11.** F
2. F	**7.** T	**12.** T
3. T	**8.** T	**13.** T
4. F	**9.** F	**14.** F
5. T	**10.** T	**15.** T

Key Terms Review

1. d	**4.** i	**7.** a
2. g	**5.** e	**8.** f
3. b	**6.** h	**9.** c

Applying Concepts

Your answer should include such advice as the following:

- Install an alarm.
- Remember to remove the keys from the ignition.
- Store the vehicle in a locked garage.
- Never leave the engine running while you go into a store.
- Install a Low-Jack system.
- Do not leave a magnetic key box anywhere on the underside of the vehicle for emergencies.
- Lock all car doors whenever you leave the car.
- Keep the windows rolled up when you are out of the vehicle.

Chapter 18

Concept Review

1.	T	**6.**	T	**11.**	T	**16.**	T
2.	F	**7.**	T	**12.**	F	**17.**	T
3.	F	**8.**	F	**13.**	T	**18.**	T
4.	T	**9.**	F	**14.**	F	**19.**	F
5.	T	**10.**	F	**15.**	F	**20.**	F

Key Terms Review

1.	h	**7.**	p	**13.**	l
2.	d	**8.**	q	**14.**	n
3.	m	**9.**	b	**15.**	a
4.	c	**10.**	i	**16.**	j
5.	k	**11.**	o	**17.**	e
6.	g	**12.**	f		

Applying Concepts

1. As already indicated, you need first to report the incident to headquarters. Next, you need to check on the identity of the man and verify that he is the manager of the theater and this is not a hoax. You should also check on the fire, if possible. Do not enter the storage room if the door or door handle is warm. It is important also to ask about ventilation in the storage room. Are there any fans, vents, open windows, and so on?

If you can extinguish the fire, do so. If not, again advise headquarters, and request additional officers and the fire department. With the assistance of the manager, have the film stopped in each theater. Explain to the patrons that a problem has arisen and everyone must leave the theater. Have people leave in as orderly a way as possible. Avoid using affected words. You might even be inventive. For example, you could tell the patrons that there is a new safety program in town and that this is a drill to see how quickly they can leave the theater. Apologize for any inconvenience.

2. Until you know otherwise, treat this package as a bomb: do not touch it. If headquarters has not already requested the bomb unit (from your department, the state police, or the local National Guard unit), do so. Request back-up officers. Do not touch, move, or in any other way disturb the package.

Have the manager make an announcement over the public address system of the store, asking people to leave their shopping carts and exit the store immediately. With the assistance of back-up officers and the manager, quickly walk up and down the aisles to make sure everyone has been evacuated. If the package is a bomb and the bomb unit arrives before it detonates, the bomb unit will handle removal. You should handle crowd control. Even if the 20 minutes elapse before the bomb unit arrives, and there is no explosion, wait for the bomb unit to remove the device.

Chapter 19

Concept Review

1. T	6. F	11. F	16. F
2. F	7. T	12. F	17. T
3. T	8. T	13. T	18. T
4. F	9. T	14. T	19. T
5. F	10. T	15. F	20. T

Key Terms Review

1. e	5. k	9. g
2. c	6. a	10. b
3. h	7. j	11. f
4. i	8. d	

Applying Concepts

1. There may be some form of smuggling or drug trafficking going on. Or the motel may be a brothel, where men stop off to have sex and then leave.
2. This could represent a money-laundering operation, in which actual sales are not important. Or it may be some type of gambling or bookmaking operation. It could also be a numbers drop for a numbers operation.
3. This fire may have been set to collect insurance money. Or it may be revenge against the owner for some wrong he may have done to another criminal group.
4. This may be a place where criminals meet to plan their activities. It may also be a location where instructions are given to lower-level members of a criminal organization.
5. This could be a pickup of protection money or of numbers slips.
6. The young men described sound like drug dealers.

Chapter 20

Concept Review

1. F	6. F	11. T
2. F	7. F	12. F
3. T	8. F	13. T
4. T	9. T	14. F
5. T	10. T	15. T

Key Terms Review

1. d	6. b	11. a
2. h	7. n	12. g
3. m	8. j	13. l
4. c	9. f	14. e
5. i	10. k	

Applying Concepts

1. This is not a case of white-collar crime. The manager was wrong to fire Johnson. The only thing Johnson is guilty of is being negligent.
2. Technically, the student is guilty of a form of white-collar crime called *mundane crime*. Although it may seem petty, she is clearly violating the office policy and consequently stealing Xerox copies.
3. In this case, Katherine Lorraine and William Bender are both committing a white-collar crime. Both are guilty, at a minimum, of embezzlement. In addition, they may be attempting to defraud the federal government of income tax owed by the company.

Chapter 21

Concept Review

1. F	**6.** T	**11.** T	**16.** F
2. T	**7.** F	**12.** T	**17.** T
3. F	**8.** F	**13.** T	**18.** T
4. T	**9.** F	**14.** T	**19.** F
5. F	**10.** F	**15.** T	**20.** T

Key Terms Review

1. e	**6.** d	**11.** h
2. a	**7.** j	**12.** k
3. i	**8.** f	**13.** b
4. g	**9.** m	
5. l	**10.** c	

Applying Concepts

1. There was probable cause for the officers to stop and investigate the situation and to question the two men. There was also probable cause for an arrest, and because the search of the vehicle was incident to the arrest of the two men, it, too, was lawful.

2. Charges against Harris Conners and Milton Jones might include a possession charge as well as flight to escape arrest and/or simple resistance of arrest.

3. The statement made by Milton Jones can be used against him in court. This is because it was a voluntary admission of guilt made before he or Conners was placed in custody or questioned.

4. The arrests were appropriate, since the officers had witnessed what they believed was a drug buy and Jones corroborated the fact with his statement. Also, the discovery of the drugs on the ground—despite Conners's denial—offers probable cause to believe that he has just purchased drugs from Jones.

Chapter 22

Concept Review

1. T	**6.** F	**11.** T
2. T	**7.** F	**12.** T
3. T	**8.** T	**13.** T
4. T	**9.** F	**14.** T
5. T	**10.** T	**15.** F

Key Terms Review

1. b	**5.** c	**9.** j
2. f	**6.** k	**10.** e
3. i	**7.** g	**11.** l
4. h	**8.** a	**12.** d

Applying Concepts

The officers can contact the manager by feigning a complaint and asking to see the manager. Together, they can then plan their course of action. Given the circumstances, the officers should have brought with them either tracking equipment or marked bills to place in the bag with the extortion money. It may not be possible to adequately clear the store, since the bomber has indicated that he can detonate the bomb by radio control. Instead, a surveillance of the money should be established, with undercover officers waiting in the parking area as well as in the store.

In addition, the local bomb unit or the state bomb squad should be notified and placed on alert at the mall. As soon as the money has been picked up, the bomb squad should move in to determine if the package contains a bomb and may be radio-controlled. Their findings will determine the next action. If it is a bomb, the surveillance should continue on the pickup person until the bomb has been neutralized. At that point, the pickup person should be arrested.